CW00566652

## MARCELO DOS SANTOS

Marcelo Dos Santos's other plays include *Lionboy* (adaptation for Complicite, UK and international tour); *Cheer Up, This is Only the Beginning* (co-writer, Liverpool Playhouse); *Knights* (Exeter Bike Shed); *Safety* (Arcola); *Moshing Lying Down* (Shunt Vaults/ festivals tour) and *Lovers Walk* (Southwark Playhouse).

He has been on attachment at the Royal Court Theatre, HighTide Theatre, and his work has been developed with the National Theatre Studio.

Marcelo is currently under commission to Lucky Giant (NBC International) to develop a new sitcom.

**Other Titles in this Series**

Mike Bartlett
BULL
GAME
AN INTERVENTION
KING CHARLES III
WILD

Tom Basden
THE CROCODILE
HOLES
JOSEPH K
THERE IS A WAR

Jez Butterworth
JERUSALEM
JEZ BUTTERWORTH PLAYS: ONE
MOJO
THE NIGHT HERON
PARLOUR SONG
THE RIVER
THE WINTERLING

Phil Davies
FIREBIRD

Marcelo Dos Santos
LIONBOY *after* Zizou Corder

Phoebe Eclair-Powell
EPIC LOVE AND POP SONGS
FURY
WINK

Vivienne Franzmann
MOGADISHU
PESTS
THE WITNESS

James Fritz
THE FALL
ROSS & RACHEL

Stacey Gregg
LAGAN
OVERRIDE
PERVE
SCORCH
SHIBBOLETH
WHEN COWS GO BOOM

Ella Hickson
THE AUTHORISED KATE BANE
BOYS
EIGHT
OIL
PRECIOUS LITTLE TALENT
    & HOT MESS
WENDY & PETER PAN *after* Barrie

Sam Holcroft
COCKROACH
DANCING BEARS
EDGAR & ANNABEL
PINK
RULES FOR LIVING
THE WARDROBE
WHILE YOU LIE

Vicky Jones
THE ONE

Anna Jordan
CHICKEN SHOP
FREAK
YEN

Lucy Kirkwood
BEAUTY AND THE BEAST
    *with* Katie Mitchell
BLOODY WIMMIN
CHIMERICA
HEDDA *after* Ibsen
IT FELT EMPTY WHEN THE
    HEART WENT AT FIRST BUT
    IT IS ALRIGHT NOW
NSFW
TINDERBOX

Ben Musgrave
CRUSHED SHELLS AND MUD
PRETEND YOU HAVE BIG
    BUILDINGS

Kathryn O'Reilly
SCREWED

Evan Placey
CONSENSUAL
GIRLS LIKE THAT
GIRLS LIKE THAT & OTHER PLAYS
    FOR TEENAGERS
PRONOUN

James Rushbrooke
TOMCAT

Stef Smith
HUMAN ANIMALS
REMOTE
SWALLOW

Jack Thorne
2ND MAY 1997
BUNNY
BURYING YOUR BROTHER IN
    THE PAVEMENT
HOPE
JACK THORNE PLAYS: ONE
LET THE RIGHT ONE IN
    *after* John Ajvide Lindqvist
MYDIDAE
THE SOLID LIFE OF SUGAR WATER
STACY & FANNY AND FAGGOT
WHEN YOU CURE ME

Phoebe Waller-Bridge
FLEABAG

Tom Wells
BROKEN BISCUITS
FOLK
JUMPERS FOR GOALPOSTS
THE KITCHEN SINK
ME, AS A PENGUIN

Marcelo Dos Santos

# NEW LABOUR

NICK HERN BOOKS

London

www.nickhernbooks.co.uk

**A Nick Hern Book**

*New Labour* first published in Great Britain in 2016 as a paperback original by Nick Hern Books Limited, The Glasshouse, 49a Goldhawk Road, London W12 8QP

*New Labour* copyright © 2016 Marcelo Dos Santos

Marcelo Dos Santos has asserted his right to be identified as the author of this work

Cover image: iStockphoto.com/Klikk

Designed and typeset by Nick Hern Books, London
Printed and bound in Great Britain by Mimeo Ltd, Huntingdon, Cambridgeshire PE29 6XX

A CIP catalogue record for this book is available from the British Library

ISBN 978 1 84842 592 7

**CAUTION**   All rights whatsoever in this play are strictly reserved. Requests to reproduce the text in whole or in part should be addressed to the publisher.

**Amateur Performing Rights**   Applications for performance, including readings and excerpts, by amateurs in English should be addressed to the Performing Rights Manager, Nick Hern Books, The Glasshouse, 49a Goldhawk Road, London W12 8QP, *tel* +44 (0)20 8749 4953, *email* rights@nickhernbooks.co.uk, except as follows:

*Australia:* Dominie Drama, 8 Cross Street, Brookvale 2100, *tel* (2) 9938 8686, *fax* (2) 9938 8695, *email* drama@dominie.com.au

*New Zealand:* Play Bureau, PO Box 9013, St Clair, Dunedin 9047, *tel* (3) 455 9959, *email* info@playbureau.com

*South Africa:* DALRO (pty) Ltd, PO Box 31627, 2017 Braamfontein, *tel* (11) 712 8000, *fax* (11) 403 9094, *email* theatricals@dalro.co.za

*United States of America and Canada:* Troika, see details below

**Professional Performing Rights**   Applications for performance by professionals in any medium and in any language throughout the world (and by amateur and stock companies in the United States of America and Canada) should be addressed to Troika, 10a Christina Street, London, EC2A 4PA, *tel* +44 (0)20 7336 7868, *web* www.troikatalent.com

No performance of any kind may be given unless a licence has been obtained. Applications should be made before rehearsals begin. Publication of this play does not necessarily indicate its availability for amateur performance.

*New Labour* was first performed at the Royal Academy of
Dramatic Art, London, in November 2014, with the following
cast:

| | |
|---|---|
| ALICE | Caroline Moroney |
| LIAM | Daniel O'Keefe |
| LIZ | Faye Wilson |
| BRIAN | Freddie Meredith |
| COLETTE | Tamara Lawrence |
| CAL | Sean Delaney |
| ROB | Rupert Lazarus |
| SALLY | Alice Robinson |
| DUNCAN | Peter Mulligan |
| *Director* | Richard Wilson |
| *Designer* | Mark Friend |

**Acknowledgements**

Thanks to: Richard Wilson, Ed Kemp, Lloyd Trott and all at RADA, Christopher Campbell, Kenneth Emson, Yates Norton, and the Nick Hern Books team.

*M.D.S.*

*For Carol and Patrick Paul McGowan*

**Characters**

ALICE
LIAM
LIZ
BRIAN
COLETTE
CAL
ROB
SALLY
ROISIN
DUNCAN

**Note on Play**

All the characters are in their early twenties, except Liz, Sally
and Duncan who are slightly older, mid-twenties; and Colette
who is slightly younger, eighteen to twenty.

**Setting**

The play is set in a call centre. The space is open plan, with an
area where they make calls to one side and a 'break out' space
with a small sofa and kitchen on the other. The original
production represented it naturalistically but it has been
produced elsewhere with minimal set.

**ACT ONE**

**Spring**

ALICE (*twenty-one, pretty, northern*) *sits entwined with* LIAM (*twenty-one, slightly geeky*) *on the sofa in the 'break out' area of the space.*

ALICE. No!

LIAM. Yes!

ALICE. You?

LIAM. Me.

ALICE. You? Liam?

LIAM (*Tarzan impression*). Me Liam, you Alice.

   *Beat.*

ALICE. Fucking hell.

LIAM. I know.

ALICE. On your own?

LIAM. Yeah.

ALICE. That's just. That's just. On your own? You're not going with Rob?

LIAM. No. I was going to go with my mate Steve from back home but he keeps bailing and I thought: fuck it.

ALICE. I can't even go to the loo on my own. South America?

LIAM. Colombia, but then Bolivia, Argentina / Peru, Brazil –

ALICE. Do you speak Spanish?

LIAM. No.

ALICE. What the fuck?

LIAM. I know.

ALICE. You?

LIAM. Yes me, why not me?

ALICE. Well you know you're not very –

LIAM. Exciting?

ALICE. Adventurous. You're my hamster, aren't you?

LIAM. I've had enough of my wheel. I'm making a break for it.

ALICE. What will you do?

LIAM. I'm going to teach in a school in Colombia.

ALICE. Oh my God are you going to save the world?

LIAM. No, obviously but I want to do something. I want to help. But after that who knows? The open road.

ALICE. Get you. The open road. You can't even drive.

LIAM. I'll learn.

ALICE. You seem different.

LIAM. I feel different.

ALICE. What do you feel?

LIAM. I feel. I feel real, you know?

ALICE. No, no I don't.

LIAM. You do.

ALICE. I don't.

LIAM. It feels good.

ALICE. I bet. (*Beat*.) Have you told anyone else yet?

LIAM. No. Just you.

*Beat.*

ALICE. I don't want you to go.

*Beat.*

LIAM. Come with me then.

ALICE. No. To Colombia? No.

LIAM. Why not?

ALICE. I can't. No money.

LIAM. Credit card.

ALICE. It's so far.

LIAM. That's what's brilliant.

ALICE. I look like a drug mule.

LIAM *laughs.*

It's true, I do. I'll get caught and end up in jail for sixty years.

LIAM. Well, just try not to smuggle cocaine.

ALICE. I know but sometimes they / sneak it into your suitcase and you don't even know it.

LIAM. Who's they?

ALICE. It's the kind of daft thing that would happen to me.

LIAM. I don't think it will.

ALICE. I can't risk it.

*She rests on him.*

I mean what would I even do?

LIAM. Work in the school with me. There's beaches and turtles. There are cities in the middle of the jungle, which are above the cloud line. Can you imagine that?

ALICE. Your face then.

LIAM. What?

ALICE. Go to Colombia, Liam. Climb a mountain. Save the children.

LIAM. Well they are our future.

ALICE. And shag Shakira for me.

LIAM. Okay, if I have to.

ALICE. You do.

*Pause.*

LIAM. I was just thinking: I've got some money saved, if you did want to go I could lend you some.

ALICE. Liam!

LIAM. It's alright. It's cheaper going with someone, you can split things.

ALICE. Don't be daft, I was just joking, you're being daft now.

LIAM. I'm not.

ALICE. What about Cal?

LIAM. What about him?

ALICE.

LIAM. Well, he could come if he wanted.

*Beat.*

ALICE *gives him a kiss on the cheek.*

ALICE. I'm proud of you, hamster.

*He smiles.*

*Enter LIZ, mid-twenties, Australian. Wild.*

LIZ (*to LIAM*). Pass her over.

LIZ *sits down and LIAM manoeuvres ALICE over to LIZ like a baby.*

Thanks, love.

LIAM *stands up and heads towards the exit.*

LIAM. I'm going to get supplies. Do you want anything in particular?

LIZ. Nah, surprise me.

> LIAM *exits*.

Such a sweetie.

ALICE. I know.

> LIZ *kisses her leg.* ALICE *laughs.*

> *She keeps kissing it, moving towards* ALICE*'s feet.*

Not my feet.

LIZ. Yes your feet.

ALICE. No, I'm all sweaty.

> *She squeals and squirms around.* LIZ *takes off* ALICE*'s pumps.*

LIZ. Oh. My. God.

ALICE. I know they stink. I said. Stop it.

LIZ. These are impossibly perfect feet.

ALICE. No! They're disgusting.

LIZ. Are you kidding? I could eat them. I want to eat them. Can I eat them? Let me eat them.

ALICE. Don't! They're manky.

LIZ. Does Cal suck your toes?

ALICE. Definitely not. He's a bit funny about stuff sometimes.

LIZ. Stuff, you say. What stuff?

ALICE. I shouldn't say.

LIZ. Well now you have to say and by the way you have to tell me everything you've ever thought or done and keep in constant radio contact, from now on yeah?

ALICE. Okay.

LIZ. I'm serious. Day or night. I'm so glad I found you.

ALICE. Me too.

LIZ. Go on. What's he funny about?

ALICE. Nothing. It's me.

LIZ. You're fucking beautiful, Alice, you know that, right?

ALICE. No I'm not.

LIZ. Shut up. What's the issue?

ALICE. I'm worried about breaking him; my thigh is bigger than his head.

LIZ. Nope, not possible, your thigh is gorgeous and non-existent and that boy has a big motherfucking head. No offence.

ALICE. He's actually really shy.

LIZ. As long as he makes you smile and sucks your toes. Does he make you smile?

*Beat.*

Dump him then.

*Offended,* ALICE *begins to move away from* LIZ.

Don't.

ALICE. Where is everyone?

LIZ. Don't. Don't fucking. Don't do that. Just live here on my lap. Just stay where you are. Just let's just stay like this. Forever.

ALICE. Forever. That would be nice.

*Beat.*

Liam's leaving.

LIZ. Fuck. What's he doing?

ALICE. Travelling.

LIZ. Sweet.

ALICE. Maybe I should travel.

LIZ. Travelling is overrated. Trust me.

ALICE. Or maybe I should get a proper job.

LIZ. You're a singer though, right? That's your job.

ALICE. Yeah but I don't really do it. I do this.

LIZ. You've just graduated, relax.

ALICE. I've been out a year.

LIZ. Be in the moment, baby, you're so young. You don't have to be anywhere yet.

ALICE *acquiesces*.

ALICE. I can't believe we've only just met.

LIZ. No, baby, no. That's just temporal time, you know. There's something deeper. There's something very old here. Something to do with souls. Do you know what I mean?

ALICE. Yes.

LIZ. Do you know what I mean?

ALICE. Yes.

LIZ. But do you know what I mean?

ALICE. Yes.

LIZ. You feel what I'm saying?

ALICE. Totally.

LIZ. Am I talking shit?

ALICE. Yes.

LIZ. I am aren't I?

ALICE. Yes.

LIZ. Maybe we should get married. What's your surname?

ALICE. Nutter.

LIZ. What?

ALICE *starts laughing*.

ALICE (*through the giggles*). Nutter. My surname is – (*Can't stop laughing*.) Nutter.

LIZ. Nutter? As in English for nuts?

ALICE. Yes.

*More laughter.*

LIZ. That is just fucking –

ALICE. I know.

LIZ. We're definitely getting married and I'm taking your name.

ALICE. Yes. As long as I can take yours and not be nuts.

LIZ. You're not crazy, baby.

*Beat.*

ALICE. You don't really know me.

LIZ. Yes I do. You are perfection. Never ever change.

ALICE *kisses her.*

*Beat.*

Those lips! The motherfucking lips.

*Enter* COLETTE.

COLETTE. Sorry.

*She goes to leave.*

LIZ. No stay.

COLETTE. Am I interrupting something?

LIZ. Nah we're just having sex.

ALICE. We're not.

LIZ. We could do. We all could do. You ever had your toes sucked, Colette?

COLETTE. No way.

LIZ. Fucking English chicks.

COLETTE. Can you smell weed?

ALICE. Shit.

LIZ. I don't know. Can you smell weed?

COLETTE. Yes.

LIZ. Interesting.

ALICE. Weird.

LIZ. A mystery.

> LIZ *touches* ALICE*'s leg*.

> Is that your leg or mine?

ALICE. I think it's mine.

LIZ. Fuck me, what's that made of?

ALICE. Sandpaper.

LIZ. Nah; baby's bum.

COLETTE. Are you guys stoned?

LIZ. Are you?

COLETTE. No.

LIZ. Do you want to be?

COLETTE. I can't believe you're stoned at work.

LIZ. Shit, are we at work?

> ALICE *laughs*.

COLETTE. Does Sally let you smoke?

LIZ. Fuck no.

ALICE. Can you imagine?

LIZ. God there's a chick that needs to get stoned. And laid. I mean I hate saying that because it's such a fucking patriarchal reading of women but my God. My God. Someone give that woman an orgasm.

COLETTE. Won't she freak out if she smells it?

LIZ. Didn't you hear the good news?

COLETTE. No.

LIZ. She's had a family emergency.

COLETTE. Oh no. Is everything okay?

LIZ. No, thank fuck. She's off for the afternoon.

COLETTE. Who's in charge?

ALICE. Brian.

COLETTE. Which one's Brian?

BRIAN. Me.

> BRIAN, *previously unseen, under a table or hiding behind a coat rack.*

> This one is Brian.

LIZ. Fuck I forgot about you, Bri. Have you been there the whole time?

BRIAN. Affirmative.

LIZ. First time Bri's ever smoked a joint. Isn't that right, Bri?

BRIAN. Affirmative.

LIZ. How's it working out for you?

BRIAN. It's had absolutely no effect on me at all.

COLETTE. Where are the others?

ALICE. Cal's in an audition.

COLETTE. What about Liam?

LIZ. Oh my God I love Liam so much.

ALICE. Me too.

LIZ. Isn't he just like the best? The nicest. So much heart. He's just a walking man-shaped heart you know what I mean? And oh my God does he fancy you.

ALICE. Shut up.

LIZ. Why aren't you with Liam?

ALICE. We're just mates and because I'm with Cal.

LIZ. Yeah yeah. Next!

ALICE. And he's not that –

LIZ. Yeah no he's not a looker. But you know he's such
a sweetie.

ALICE. Why aren't you with him?

LIZ. Oh my God why aren't I with him? Because I'm seeing
this super-hot DJ who is literally ruining my life and driving
me insane and that's what I do.

ALICE. That's what I do.

LIZ. That's what you do but it's not who you are. It's not your
truth. Marry Liam. He's such an old soul. Isn't he an old soul?

COLETTE. Have they gone home?

LIZ. Nah, think he's out getting supplies.

COLETTE (*alarmed*). What kind of supplies?

LIZ. Calm down, Col, we're not talking crack cocaine.

COLETTE. I should get on with work.

ALICE. It's not even two.

COLETTE. It's fine, I don't mind.

LIZ. What's your deal, Col?

COLETTE. Colette. Nothing. I'm just worried about getting
behind if we don't start soon.

LIZ. Why?

COLETTE. Because there's targets and they monitor the calls.

LIZ. Brian monitors the calls.

BRIAN. And you're all doing really well.

ALICE. Brian, you're the cutest.

BRIAN. Back of the net.

COLETTE. But we'll have to make some calls.

LIZ. We'll make some calls, don't worry. We'll just have some fun doing it for once.

COLETTE. I don't do drugs.

LIZ. Are you religious?

COLETTE. My family are.

LIZ. What about you?

COLETTE. That's quite personal. You're quite personal aren't you?

LIZ (*annoyed*). Does personal mean real, human, open? If it does then yes I'm fucking personal.

ALICE (*warning*). Liz.

*Beat.*

LIZ. How old are you?

COLETTE. Nineteen.

LIZ. Oh baby.

*Beat.*

Oh my God I'm sorry, you're a baby.

*She gets up and hugs* COLETTE, *who is stiff in her embrace.*

No don't be scared, baby. I'm going to look after you.

COLETTE. I'm fine, thanks.

LIZ. No, baby. You're too young to be fine. You should be fucking joyful or totally suicidal. Why aren't you at uni?

COLETTE. I'm saving up.

LIZ. Beautiful. That's beautiful. Do you like it here?

COLETTE.

LIZ. The correct answer is no.

COLETTE. It's fine.

LIZ *lets her go.*

LIZ. Alright. No worries, we'll keep it down.

*Beat.*

Jeez.

COLETTE. I'm not being rude. I just can't get fired.

LIZ. No one's getting fired. Baby, listen to me. This place is
not fine, this place is unbearable. Just the worst. Believe me,
I've worked in so many fucking shitholes. I've cleaned
brothels in Blackpool okay and this place. This shitty place
and the shit that we have to say is just the worst. What do we
have? Thirty minutes for lunch, twenty minutes in the
afternoon and forty-five seconds between fucking godawful,
soul-destroying calls to live in. This is a gift. This afternoon
is a gift. It may never happen again, so you've got to take it.
You have to take it with both hands. Take it.

*Pause.*

COLETTE. I'll see.

LIZ. Beautiful.

COLETTE. I'll see how it goes.

LIZ. May I kiss your hands?

COLETTE. What?

LIZ. Can I kiss your hands?

ALICE. Take the offer, she wanted to kiss my feet earlier.

COLETTE. Okay.

LIZ *kisses* COLETTE*'s hands.*

BRIAN. What about me?

LIZ. Bri, I will kiss your elbow, get it out.

*He rolls up his shirt sleeve.*

Surprisingly supple, Bri, do you moisturise?

BRIAN. What?

LIZ. Do you moisturise your elbow?

BRIAN. What? Moisturise? Why? Why would you moisturise your elbow?

*BRIAN laughs. Can't stop laughing.*

LIZ. Girls moisturise everywhere, Bri.

ALICE. You okay, Brian?

BRIAN (*through the laughter*)....elbows.

LIZ. Jesus, Bri, you're the best fucking audience.

*CAL enters.*

CAL. Hey.

ALICE. There's my lover.

*She runs over to him and kisses him.*

CAL. Have you been smoking weed?

ALICE. Just a bit.

CAL. In here?

ALICE. No we did it on the terrace. It's Liz's.

CAL. Let's have another one then.

LIZ. Jeez which charm school did you go to? Ps and Qs, darling.

CAL (*fake gangster*). Roll one up, bitch.

ALICE. How was the audition?

CAL. Alright.

ALICE. Cal's up for a film.

COLETTE. That's exciting. What's the film?

CAL. I don't want to talk about it.

COLETTE. Oh, okay.

CAL. Sorry, it's just, you know. Pressure.

LIZ (*putting the boot in*). Oh well better luck next time.

CAL. It actually went quite well, thanks.

LIZ (*fake sincere*). Great. Really pleased.

CAL. What's happening here?

> *Enter* LIAM *clinking with bottles of vodka and small bottles of Coke.*

LIAM. We iz happening.

> *He holds aloft the booze.*

> Yo yo yo.

BRIAN. Yo yo yo Liam in the house.

LIAM. Brian in da house representing da management.

BRIAN. Check it.

LIZ. We were just saying how we've got the hots for you.

LIAM (*fake Australian*). Oh yeah.

LIZ (*parodying her own accent*). Oh my gawd are you saying I sound bogan. I'm fucking posh me... But no totally we think you're hunk city.

LIAM. I doubt that very much but thank you, ladies. You alright, Cal?

CAL. Yeah. You?

LIAM. How was the audition?

CAL (*to* ALICE). Did you tell everyone about it?

ALICE. No.

CAL. Don't tell people, okay?

ALICE. Okay.

> ALICE *turns away and goes back towards* LIZ.

LIAM. She's just proud of you, mate.

CAL. Whatever, it was just an audition.

> *Enter* ROB.

ROB. Boom and he's here.

> *No one really responds.*

LIAM. Hey, Rob.

ROB. Bit of an underwhelming response. I'll try again. Boom and he's here.

BRIAN. Boom!

ROB. Good effort, Bri. Liam. Have you heard about Sally?

LIAM. Yep. I'm on it.

> LIAM *holds up the booze.*

ROB. There we go. There you are. Here we are, let's drink.

LIZ. Fuck yeah!

ROB. Okay, these are the rules. Drink every time they say sorry.

BRIAN. Drink every time they ask how much?

LIZ. Drink every time they say recession.

CAL. Drink every time they say to call back.

LIAM. Drink every time they swear at you.

ALICE. Drink when they say it's a bad line.

LIZ. And then drink every time they say no.

> BRIAN *starts pouring vodka into their water bottles and Coke bottles throughout the following.*

COLETTE. That's all they've said so far.

LIAM. You don't have to drink.

LIZ. You totally have to drink.

COLETTE. What if we get caught?

ROB. Who's going to catch us? Brian's in charge.

BRIAN. I'm in charge.

ROB. Yes, buddy, you're in charge.

BRIAN. Who's the boss?

LIZ. You're the boss.

BRIAN. Back of the net!

COLETTE. I'll see how I go.

ALICE (*to* CAL). Are you going to play?

CAL. Maybe.

ALICE. Maybe I shouldn't.

CAL. Do it if you want.

ALICE. I shouldn't, I'm not feeling great.

CAL. Don't then.

ALICE. But are you?

CAL. Yes.

COLETTE. Well if Alice isn't going to do it.

ALICE. No, I'm doing it. It's fine. Don't worry. It'll be fun.

LIZ. Everyone ready?

ALICE. Yes. Wait. I just need to go to the toilet.

CAL. Hurry up.

COLETTE. I'm going to go as well.

CAL. Fucking hell.

BRIAN. Girls and their bladders, eh?

ALICE. Shut up, Bri.

ALICE *and* COLETTE *exit in search of the toilet.*

LIZ. Fucking girls. Fucking women, yeah? Thank Christ it's just us lads.

*She swigs her drink.*

So, Cal, Alice tells me you won't suck her toes, what's up with that?

CAL. I don't know what you're talking about.

LIZ. I feel like you might be into really specific stuff like a little Japanese man who wants to be dressed up like a small child and suckled.

CAL. What the fuck?

ROB (*to* LIZ). Bet you're up for weird shit.

LIZ. Why, you offering?

ROB. Of course. Any time. Now. Men's toilets, five minutes.

LIZ. Aw are you into piss, Rob? Thing about piss-play is you have to be very secure. It's really not for the first date. You need a lot of trust, a lot of intimacy and you need to be a fucking grown-up, do you know what I mean? Because after it's over you're going to have to look at each other in the eye. And if you can be like: 'I love you even more, you are awesome', then great. But if you've got your own shit or they've got their own shit then it's not going to work out, and you're just going to feel like shit. FYI same for shit-play.

*Beat.*

ROB. Fucking hell, Liz, you're dirt.

LIZ. I'm sex positive, thank you,

ROB. You're literally the dirtiest girl I know and I'm from Essex.

LIZ. How many fingers?

ROB. What?

LIZ. How many fingers?

ROB. What?

*She makes a gesture with her hand involving a couple of fingers.*

No way.

LIZ. Don't lie of course you've done it.

ROB. Two. No more than two.

LIZ. Ah fuck off, you could take more than two.

ROB. No way.

LIZ. Cal?

CAL. Not playing.

LIZ. That's what I'm hearing.

CAL. What does that mean?

BRIAN. What are we talking about?

ROB. What, mate, have you still not gone digital?

LIZ. I think it's pretty safe to assume that Bri's got a tight little anus? What you want to do is get a dildo just a small one at first and then work at it a bit, you're probably not working up to it enough, Brian.

BRIAN. Bums against the walls, lads.

LIZ. And you've got to lube. Remember to lube, kids.

*Enter* COLETTE *and* ALICE.

COLETTE. We're back but we're going to take it steady.

ROB. Fine, and one, two, three.

*They start the calls.*

Hello, this is Rob –

COLETTE. Good afternoon, my name is Colettte.

LIAM. Hello there, I'm Liam.

LIZ. Liz.

CAL. Cal.

ALICE. Hello, good afternoon, I'm Alice.

BRIAN. I'm Bri and it's Fri.

ROB. I'm calling in regards to an expression of interest you or someone in your household made –

COLETTE. With regards to a makeover and photoshoot. It would have been in the Bullring Shopping Centre. You signed up saying you might be interested in a professional makeover and photoshoot.

CAL. No don't worry…

*He holds up his bottle and drinks.*

But perhaps I can speak to you, perhaps this could be a surprise gift for Tracey.

LIAM. We have several offers and they're all very reasonable thanks for asking.

*He drinks.*

ROB. Professional, editorial photographer, stylist which as far as I'm concerned is just a fancy word for hairdresser. They do you over basically. No not like that unless you pay more, darling.

CAL. No I completely understand but can I just ask you a question?

COLETTE. What do you think a reasonable price might be?

CAL. What are you getting your wife for Christmas?

CAL *drinks.*

ALICE. No, okay, that's fine. Nice to talk to you. Thank you for your time.

*She takes a big gulp.*

LIAM. We can send you a catalogue but do you have access to the internet?

*He drinks.*

LIZ. Oh look I know this bloody recession.

*She drinks.*

COLETTE. Thank you for your time.

LIAM. Well, I could talk to your granddaughter but wouldn't it be a nice surprise?

LIZ. I'm from Australia, yeah. Good spotting.

BRIAN. – a whole day of pampering really.

*He drinks.*

*They drink.*

CAL. Thanks for your time.

BRIAN. No, that's a-okay, nice talking to you, sir.

LIZ. No don't worry, you're not being rude. It's been lovely talking to you.

*She drinks.*

LIAM. Great. I'll just need to get your details. No of course I can wait, it's the long number at the front.

And the expiry date.

And the last three digits on the back. That's gone through now. Yes I know. I've got your address so we'll just send you everything you need in the post. Yes absolutely, the old-fashioned way.

BRIAN. Nice one, mate.

LIAM. Thanks.

*Silence.*

ALICE. Fuck.

LIAM. You alright?

ALICE. Let's get fucked.

*She swigs her drink.*

\*\*\*

*Time has elapsed. Drink has been drunk. CAL, ALICE and
LIAM on the small sofa which is to one side of the room.
COLETTE dances on her own in another, perhaps listening
to music on her iPod. The others are out smoking. CAL is
listening to a message on his phone.*

ALICE. Am I fucked, Cal?

CAL. Yes.

ALICE. Am I too fucked, Cal?

CAL.

ALICE. Am I too fucked?

CAL.

ALICE. Cal?

CAL. What?

ALICE. Why are you being like this?

LIAM. My cue.

CAL. No, mate, stay, I've got to ring my agent.

*CAL gets up.*

*ALICE gets up.*

ALICE. Where are you going?

CAL. To call my agent.

ALICE. Where are you going?

CAL. I fucking said.

ALICE. Cal?

CAL. What?

ALICE. Why are you being such a cunt to me?

*CAL goes to her and kisses her on the forehead. She melts into his arms.*

I'm sorry.

CAL. It's okay. I'll be back in a minute.

ALICE. Where are you going?

CAL. I said. I fucking said. (*More patiently.*) Okay?

ALICE. Oh no.

CAL. What?

ALICE. I've ruined it.

CAL. I'll be back in a minute.

ALICE. I've ruined it, haven't I?

*She buries herself in his arms.*

CAL (*to* LIAM). Mate?

LIAM. I'll go.

CAL. No, can you just give me a hand; look after her while I do this?

LIAM. Sure.

*CAL tries to pass her to LIAM.*

*ALICE pushes him off.*

ALICE. I'm alright. I'm fucking alright, ay?

*She sits down.*

*CAL exits.*

LIAM (*to* ALICE). Do you want some water?

ALICE. Oh God you're nice, Liam. Why aren't I with you?

LIAM. I don't know.

ALICE. But we're mates.

LIAM. Yeah.

ALICE. And that's better.

LIAM. Oh yeah much better.

ALICE (*referring to* CAL). He's shy.

LIAM. Is he?

ALICE. He hates it when I get drunk. He says I get lairy I don't get lairy do I?

LIAM. Yeah you do.

ALICE. Oh no, do I?

LIAM. But you're funny too.

ALICE. Thank you. You're funny.

LIAM. Yeah I know.

ALICE. He's such a dick.

LIAM. Don't say that.

ALICE. Why not, he is?

LIAM. Because you don't mean it.

ALICE. I do.

LIAM. Why are you with him then?

ALICE. He makes me happy.

*She collapses on to him somehow, clearly not happy.*

LIAM. Are you okay?

ALICE. Me? I'm fine, I'm just daft.

LIAM. You really should quit you know.

ALICE. I can't.

LIAM. You can.

ALICE. So broke. I'm borrowing off my sister.

LIAM. Work anywhere else, just go. Work in a bar.

ALICE. I've done that. Pubs aren't good for me. (*Beat.*) No it's alright, I'm alright here. Liz is nice, Cal's here. Today was fun.

LIAM. Listen to me, Liz is a flake and Cal's a dick.

ALICE. Liam! You can't say that.

LIAM. Promise me you'll get out of here.

ALICE. Of course.

LIAM. No, really. I've worked in shit places like this for years, all through uni and when I moved to London I thought, well I thought a lot of shit really, I thought I could intern for a bit and then get a job, as if I could just walk into an NGO with a poxy degree from Essex, you need an MA just to intern. And so I ended here, same shit job, different city. You get used to a place because you think everything's going to be okay, that it's just this week or this month that's, you know, and then suddenly there's this sort of worm or something that starts wriggling around eating into all the fucking hope. There's only so much hope, you know, and you can't waste it. Don't waste it. You have talent. You're going to be a brilliant, famous singer.

ALICE. Shut up.

LIAM. You've got a beautiful voice.

ALICE. Loads of people have nice voices. I'm not special.

LIAM. Sing something.

ALICE. No I can't.

LIAM. Sing.

ALICE. I can't. I'm still drunk.

LIAM. Perfect. Don't be a wuss. Sing.

ALICE. I can't.

LIAM. You can. (*Beat.*) You can.

ALICE. Alright.

*She sings something and it's rather beautiful even if it's not perfect.*

Was that okay?

LIAM. I'm not expert but that seemed special to me.

*Beat.*

ALICE *tries to kiss* LIAM.

*He responds. They kiss.*

*She pushes him back.*

ALICE (*laughing it off*). Liam!

LIAM. Alice – (*Tries to kiss her some more.*)

ALICE. Stop it. Don't be so daft. Cal could have walked in.

LIAM *gets up annoyed.*

Are you annoyed, Liam? You're not annoyed, are you?

LIAM. No, I'm fine.

ALICE. Don't be annoyed, hamster.

LIAM. I'm not.

ALICE. You are. I can tell by the way you puff those pouches in your cheeks.

LIAM. Stop doing that.

ALICE. What am I doing?

LIAM. You know what you're doing.

*Beat.*

ALICE. You're too good for me, Liam.

LIAM. That's bullshit.

ALICE. I'm sorry.

LIAM. You're actually full of shit, Alice.

ALICE. I know. I'm sorry.

LIAM. Don't be sorry. Just fucking do something, okay?

LIAM *exits*.

ALICE. Liam!

*She chases after him.*

*A phone rings.*

COLETTE *is still dancing on her own.*

*The phone stops.*

BRIAN *and* ROB *enter and start dancing with* COLETTE. *There's no actual music.*

ROB (*to* COLETTE). You alright? Having fun?

COLETTE. I'm having loads of fun.

ROB. What we dancing to?

COLETTE. Kelis.

ROB *sings the first line of 'Milkshake' by Kelis.*

COLETTE *laughs.*

ROB. It's Michael Jackson for me, forever and always.

*He does the moonwalk.*

I don't care if he's a paedo. That man is eternal. What are you listening to, Bri Bri?

BRIAN. No idea but it's very fast.

*He has a drum-and-bass freakout in a corner.*

ROB. Brian's epic.

COLETTE. Is he a bit?

ROB. Oh yeah definitely riding high on the spectrum. Totally annoying seventy per cent of the time but show him a bit of love and he's your gimp forever. Isn't that right, squire?

BRIAN. What's that, serfling?

ROB. Bit of a gimp, aren't you?

BRIAN. No you're my gimp, serf. I'm the squire, I'm the boss today.

ROB. Yeah but you know what these aristocrats are like, they love a good spanking. Bend over.

BRIAN. Kiss my elbow.

ROB. No, Bri, we're not doing that.

BRIAN. Kiss my elbow.

ROB. What's wrong with you, mate? Showing me up in front of the new girl. Woman. Lady.

COLETTE. It's alright.

ROB. No it's properly funny. Come on, mate. Back of the net.

BRIAN. I'm dancing.

COLETTE. He's dancing.

ROB. Just fucking bend over and show us your ass.

BRIAN. I'm the boss today.

ROB. No I'm the fucking boss.

COLETTE. Stop it.

> ROB *grabs* BRIAN *and tries to put him over his knee as* LIAM *returns with some water.*

LIAM. Rob! What you doing, mate?

ROB. Master and gimp. Colette hasn't seen it.

COLETTE. I don't want to. Please stop.

LIAM. Yeah just leave it out, fella, yeah?

ROB. Just having a laugh.

LIAM (*firm*). Let him go.

ROB. Oooh, don't get your knickers in one, mate.

*But* ROB *does let* BRIAN *go.*

COLETTE. Are you okay?

BRIAN. Affirmative.

ROB. Of course he is. He loves it.

*ROB shows some kind of affection for* BRIAN, *wraps his arm around him.*

*The phone rings again.*

LIAM. Is no one going to bloody answer that?

*LIAM answers the phone.*

Oh hi. Is everything okay? Oh right. Oh no. Okay. No I didn't. Everyone must have been busy on calls. No worries, see you in a minute.

*He puts down the phone.*

Get everything out and everyone in. Sally's downstairs.

ROB. Fuck.

COLETTE. I knew this was going to happen. What do we do?

LIAM. Get Liz. Where's Liz?

*COLETTE runs out, looking for* LIZ.

BRIAN. Oh dear. Oh dear. This isn't good for Brian.

LIAM. Don't worry, we're going to be okay, Brian. She's not going to know.

*He frantically picks up all the bottles and throws them in the bin. They stick out of the bin so he gives the bin to* ROB.

Put this in the gents and find Cal and Alice.

*ROB exits.*

BRIAN. Sally will tell Duncan. Duncan will fire Brian. This is bad for Brian.

BRIAN *wails and kicks something*.

LIAM. Just sit down, Brian, at your desk and breathe. Yeah? Just count your breaths.

BRIAN *sits down at his desk and counts his breath through the following*.

ALICE *enters*.

ALICE. I'm so sorry, Liam. I'm a dick and my stomach hurts.

LIAM. Let's just get you to your desk.

ALICE. I'm going to change. I'm going to do something, I promise.

LIAM. Got to get back to work.

ALICE. Work? I can't do any more calls, my stomach hurts.

LIAM. We're nearly there. Just a couple more for Sally.

ALICE. Sally?

*Enter* LIZ *and* COLETTE.

LIZ. Fuuuuuuuuck.

LIAM. Just a bit.

ROB *reappears with* CAL.

ALICE. Lover?

CAL. Fuck.

LIAM. We all in? Okay and everyone pretend they're on a call.

*This should all happen all at once*.

ROB. Professional, editorial photographer, stylist, which as far as I'm concerned is just a fancy word for hairdresser.

LIZ. Oh yeah I know bloody recession.

CAL. Have you got access to internet?

*Enter* SALLY.

SALLY. Hello. Everything okay, Brian?

BRIAN *makes a whip-cracking sound.*

Good.

CAL. That's the long number on the front.

LIZ. Yes I am Australian. Queensland originally and then just about everywhere else.

CAL. And the three digits on the back.

LIAM. Are you okay, Sally? Hope everything's alright with your family.

SALLY. Oh. I don't. We don't. Sorry.

Not really.

*The gang stop pretending for a moment and then carry on.*

LIAM. I'm sorry.

SALLY. No, it's fine just give me a minute.

SALLY *starts to leave the room.*

ROB *does a 'get in' gesture.*

LIAM (*sotto voce*). Everyone just keep calm, but I think it's going to be okay.

ALICE *pukes everywhere, just as* SALLY *re-enters.*

**ACT TWO**

**Summer**

**Scene One**

SALLY*'s office. In the background we see* BRIAN, ROB *and* COLETTE *making calls. The rule is we don't hear all the calls except their last lines which punctuate (or perhaps run under)* ROISIN *and* SALLY*'s dialogue.*

ROISIN. Okay, that was great but can you remember to say 'Alice'.

SALLY. What did I say?

ROISIN. You said 'her'. It's just easier in the edit if you say her name. You're doing great.

BRIAN (*on a call*). The only thing I would say about taking time to think about it is that our deals change all the time. When would be a good time to call back, Mr Turner. Mr Turner?

SALLY. Am I sweating?

ROISIN (*fiddling with her camera*). What's that?

SALLY. I don't want to be shiny. They're always too shiny in these things.

ROISIN. Sorry. What was that?

SALLY. The normal people in these things, they're always shiny and sweaty. Cut from Cheryl Cole to a sweaty blob in a scout hut somewhere pumping her fat arms shouting: 'Go, Alice, we believe in you.'

ROISIN. Oh right. No you look grand.

SALLY. You just want to scream at them: 'Put some powder on your face and why did you wear that top without the sleeves, you silly mare?'

ROISIN (*still fiddling with the camera, not really listening*). Right.

SALLY. Bugger, why did I wear this top?

ROISIN. It's nice.

SALLY. I look like a middle-aged woman at a wedding.

ROISIN. You look lovely.

SALLY. I wouldn't wear this normally. This right here is my mother's doing.

ROISIN. You'll only really be on screen for fifteen seconds max. It's all about Alice really.

SALLY. Well, that's something.

COLETTE (*on a call*). Fifty's not getting on. Was he with TfL for long? Yeah that is difficult but these things have a way of working out, don't they? How old am I? I'm nineteen. Haha I don't feel young. Alright. Mrs Elufowjo. No that's fine. Lovely chatting to you.

She was nice.

SALLY. What are her chances of getting through?

ROISIN. Sorry, really annoying but I can't really talk about it.

SALLY. But it's a good sign you're here?

ROISIN. Sorry, really annoying I know.

SALLY. She's very good. Have you heard her?

ROISIN. I think so. Is she a bit Lily Allen?

SALLY. Not really.

ROISIN. Did she do the Katy Perry? What am I talking about, they all do Katy Perry.

SALLY. I think she was doing a Billie Holiday song.

ROISIN. Oh great, that's great. She's great. (*Beat*.) I mean it's hard to keep track. It's such a big operation there are literally dozens of little me's running around the country doing these.

SALLY. I see.

ROISIN. It's all about the live audition though. It's amazing what that pressure does to people, people you think will go really far and they just fall apart.

SALLY. And whether she has 'star quality' of course.

ROISIN. Oh no she's pretty enough.

*Beat*.

SALLY. Can I just put some more powder on my face?

*She starts putting on powder.*

ROISIN. Sure, absolutely but we do need to get on –

ROB. Did you see the match last night? No? Neither did I. Okay, no I get you. I'll ring back another time. What time would – ?

COLETTE *gets up and heads towards* SALLY*'s office and taps on the half-open door.*

COLETTE. Morning. (*To* ROISIN, *excitedly but shy*.) Hi.

ROISIN. Hi.

COLETTE. Can I come in?

SALLY. Sorry, Colette, can / you just give us a minute.

ROISIN. No it's fine we're ready.

SALLY (*tetchy*). Are we?

ROISIN (*to* SALLY). As long as that's okay with you?

SALLY. What about the script?

ROISIN. It sounds grand. Let's head out.

SALLY. You want to do it out there?

ROISIN. Oh I think so, don't you? It's a bit dark and gloomy in here.

SALLY. Yes I suppose it is.

ROISIN. And it would be great to get everyone involved a bit.

SALLY. You want me to say it in front of everyone.

ROISIN. But if you need more.

    SALLY *hesitates*.

SALLY. No it's fine. In fact it would be good if this didn't take up the whole day.

ROISIN. God no. (*To* COLETTE.) Hi, I'm Roisin.

COLETTE. I'm Colette. This is so exciting.

ROISIN. Do you watch the show?

COLETTE. Of course.

ROISIN. Cool.

COLETTE. I love it.

ROISIN. Cool.

COLETTE. I mean I actually love it. I even liked it when Simon wasn't in it because it was more about the contestants but I'm also really pleased he's coming back. Oh my God do you know Simon?

ROISIN. A bit, he doesn't have much to do with us but I've met him a few times. Terrifying no I mean he's lovely really nice.

COLETTE. Are you going to interview everyone?

ROISIN. No, I'm sorry, just Sally and Alice.

COLETTE (*disappointed*). Oh.

ROISIN. Where do you sit?

COLETTE. I normally sit over there.

ROISIN. And where does Alice sit?

COLETTE. Over there.

ROISIN. Maybe we could move you around so you're next to her and get you a bit more air time?

SALLY. That might be a bit difficult.

ROISIN. Why's that?

SALLY. Brian sits there.

COLETTE (*to* ROISIN). Brian's a bit funny.

ROISIN. Honestly this will literally take no time. No time. We'll quickly run through your bit, Sally, and then I'll just do some GVs of Alice at work and then I'll be out of your hair. Phew.

*She walks out of the office into the call-centre section.*

Hi, everyone, I'm Roisin I'm from a production company called –

SALLY. They're still on calls.

ROISIN. I'm so sorry. How long with they be?

SALLY. However long they need to be to make the sale.

ROISIN. Honestly, I'm in and out.

ROB (*on the phone*). Photographic makeovers, that's right. Must have been your wife, sir.

BRIAN (*on the phone*). Okedoke, well look let's just put you down for that package and then if the rest of the family isn't keen you can just get your shots done. Jolly good. Yes I know I am jolly.

SALLY *motions to* ROB *and* BRIAN *to wrap it up*.

SALLY. The sales have to come first.

ROISIN. Of course but honestly this will –

ROB (*as he gets off the call*). Fucking bust. Hi, I'm Rob, how's it going?

BRIAN (*still on the phone*). Yes this is the money bit. Just the long number on the back.

SALLY. Shh, Brian's making a sale.

*They look at* BRIAN.

BRIAN (*on the phone*). And the security code, yep three numbers on the back, very good. There that's all gone through for you now. You can expect a confirmation letter and brochure in the post and then it's just a matter of booking your appointment once you've spoken to everyone in the family. Lovely. Yes jolly good. Yes you too.

Back of the net!

SALLY. Back of the net, Brian. Well done.

BRIAN. Thank you. Just doing my job. Hi, I'm Bri. It's short for Brian.

SALLY. Brian, this is –

ROISIN. Roisin, so nice to meet you. So nice to meet you all. So I was just saying to Sally, this is going to be all very quick, just a bit of an interview with Sally some shots of you doing your thang. It's going to be really fun.

ROB. Are we getting paid for this?

ROISIN. Afraid not. In fact there are some forms I'm going to have to run around and get you to fill in at the end.

ROB. Is this going to cost us anything?

ROISIN. I'm sorry?

ROB. I mean, are you going to dock us for the time we're not working, Sal?

*They look at* SALLY.

*She hesitates.*

SALLY. No. Of course not.

ROB (*to* ROISIN). Good, in that case take as long as you like, love.

SALLY. No I didn't say that.

ROB. I need a wazz.

SALLY. Don't be long.

ROB *exits*.

BRIAN. Tea for Brian. Tea for Roisin?

ROISIN. Yes thanks, Brian.

BRIAN. You can call me Bri. It's shorter.

ROISIN. Okay.

COLETTE. And it's just you?

ROISIN. Yep just me.

SALLY. Yes I thought they'd be more.

COLETTE. I thought it would be a whole crew.

ROISIN. Not at this stage; too many contestants. There's literally dozens of little me's running around the country.

SALLY. Yes you said. Little you's?

COLETTE. Are you a producer?

ROISIN. Shooting AP.

SALLY. AP?

ROISIN. Sorry, the AP is short for assistant producer.

COLETTE. The shooting is the filming.

SALLY (*dry*). Yes I know that.

COLETTE (*to* ROISIN). Did you study TV?

ROISIN. No, it doesn't really work like that.

COLETTE. Does it not?

ROISIN. Literally no one I know who works in the industry ever really studies it at college, everyone did crazy things like Norse Studies or PPE.

COLETTE. I did media at A level.

ROISIN. Oh right. Yeah no people do come in that way too.

COLETTE. I made a music video for my media A level, it was quite good. Maybe I could get a job on the *X-Factor.*

ROISIN. You could.

COLETTE. As if.

ROISIN. Of course you could.

SALLY  How did you get in then?

ROISIN. Work experience, I was a bit lucky because my godfather works in the BBC –

SALLY. Well there you go.

ROISIN. Sure, you need contacts but once you're in you're in.

COLETTE. I don't have any contacts.

*ROISIN hands out her card.*

ROISIN. Take my card.

COLETTE. Really?

ROISIN. Email me your CV and I'll pass it on.

COLETTE. Really?

ROISIN. Of course. Why not?

COLETTE. Oh my God. Thank you. That would be so cool.

*She takes the card.*

ROISIN. It is very competitive though and I had to do a lot of work experience before I even got a running gig, just so you know…

COLETTE *looks at the card. Hands it back.*

COLETTE. No, it's okay.

ROISIN. I don't want to discourage you if you're interested. Is it something you're interested in though?

COLETTE. Yeah but there's no chance is there?

ROISIN. If it's something you really want then why not?

COLETTE. Because it won't happen.

ROISIN. How do you know?

COLETTE. Well it just won't, will it? And it's not stable. Thank you though.

*Beat.*

ROISIN. Fine. Right well any time you're ready, Sally.

SALLY *finishes putting make-up on her face.*

SALLY. Great, now I look like a corpse.

ROISIN. Honestly you look gorgeous.

SALLY. Gorgeous?

ROISIN. Honestly.

SALLY. You really don't have to say that.

ROISIN. I'm not. You are.

SALLY. Actually sorry, can you not say it please.

*Beat.*

ROISIN. Oh, I'm sorry.

*Pause.*

SALLY. No, I'm sorry it's the nerves. 'We're so proud of… (*Deliberate.*) Alice.'

ROISIN. Perfect.

SALLY. 'She's a great employee and we'd be sad to lose her but she's also such a talented singer and she deserves. She deserves…'

ROB *re-enters.*

ROB. She deserves to be a 'star' or at the very least, make a dodgy covers album and end up in Southend panto with The Krankies. Are you demanding your own lighting state, Sally?

SALLY. Of course.

BRIAN. Have you got your best angle worked out?

SALLY. Yes the back of my head.

ROISIN. No you look gorgeous. Doesn't she look gorgeous? Honestly I'm looking at you now in the camera and you look beautiful. Doesn't she have beautiful eyes?

COLETTE. Really pretty.

SALLY. Please don't.

ROISIN. You look really good on camera.

BRIAN. Sally used to be an actress.

SALLY. Brian!

ROB. Were you? You weren't.

BRIAN. She was. Well she was in *Casualty*.

COLETTE. Oh my God you were in *Casualty*.

SALLY. For two minutes. It wasn't anything.

BRIAN. She was knocked unconscious by a falling tin of paint.

ROB. She was what?

BRIAN. She was very good. She looked genuinely surprised when the tin landed on her head which I remember thinking at the time must be quite difficult as I assume they had to drop it on her head several times to get it just right.

ROB. Is that on YouTube? Can I find it on YouTube? I have to find it now.

BRIAN. How many times did they drop it on your head, Sally?

ROB. When was this?

BRIAN. A couple of years ago. Sally's mum had people round and we watched it on the telly. She kept crying didn't she, Sally?

ROB. Can't find it under 'falling tin can *Casualty*'.

SALLY (*hard*). Right. Everyone sit down and get on with your work.

*Sensing her tone, the group settle down.*

(*Mechanical, fast.*) 'We're so proud of Alice. She's a great employee and we'd be sad to lose her but she has a great voice and deserves to be a star. Go Alice.' That sort of thing.

BRIAN. Bit fast, Sally.

SALLY. I'm just getting the lines.

BRIAN. Don't forget to breathe.

SALLY. Shut the fuck up, Brian.

ROB. Ouch.

SALLY. Sorry. Actually can I just stop for a minute?

*Moving towards an exit.*

ROISIN. Is anything wrong?

SALLY. No, I, I just need a minute.

ROB. She's got to find her character. And her career.

SALLY. Fuck off, Rob.

*She exits.*

BRIAN. I think you upset her, Rob.

ROB. I think you might be right, Bri. Give a shit, I do not.

COLETTE. You're a proper knob, Rob.

ROB (*to* ROISIN). I'm not. Honestly. She's just a pain in the arse. Been here way too long. Proper nightmare control-freak boss. Not that that matters now.

BRIAN. Did you get the job?

ROB. I should bloody hope so after that interview. Honestly it wasn't an interview it was a fucking performance. They were holding back the tears, mate.

BRIAN. When do you hear?

ROB. Today. (*To* ROISIN.) Right, so where do you want me?

ROISIN. Where do you sit normally?

ROB. Back here.

ROISIN. That's fine. You stay there.

ROB. I'll try not to take that personally, love.

COLETTE (*to* ROISIN). Do you need a hand?

ROISIN. No but can we get you over here?

*She points to* BRIAN'*s chair.*

BRIAN. Sorry, that's my chair.

ROISIN. I know but just for the sake of the shot we might need to mix things up a bit.

BRIAN. I sit next to Alice.

ROISIN. Everyone will be in shot, don't worry.

BRIAN. But where will I sit?

ROISIN. Where Colette normally sits, I guess. Is everyone here yet?

BRIAN. You'll have to speak to Sally.

ROISIN. I did. She's okay with it.

BRIAN. I'm going to have to speak to Sally, then. She hasn't spoken to me.

ROISIN. Honestly, love, it's only going to take a minute.

BRIAN. She hasn't spoken to me. No one has spoken to me.

COLETTE. She's speaking to you now, Bri.

ROB. Yeah don't go off on one, mate.

BRIAN. I'm actually a supervisor here. I don't know if Sally told you that.

ROISIN. No she didn't.

BRIAN. So with respect you can just, you know, fuck off.

ROB. Mate.

COLETTE (*to* ROISIN). Sorry about him.

ROISIN. No it's fine. It doesn't matter. That's your chair, Brian. You sit there, it's not a biggie.

Look, everyone, just relax and have fun. This should be fun for you guys, okay? Enjoy it.

ALICE, *and* LIZ *enter.* ALICE *is made up and wearing a cool 1950s vintage dress.*

LIZ. Ta-dah.

*Whoops and claps from the gang.*

COLETTE. I love that dress.

ALICE. Thanks, Col.

LIZ. It's killer, right?

ALICE (*to* ROISIN). Do I look okay?

ROISIN. You look so pretty. Honestly, gorgeous.

ALICE. Thank you.

ROB. Gorgeous.

ROISIN. Thing is. Sorry, this is so annoying. I know I'm so annoying but –

ALICE. Is there something wrong?

ROISIN. No it's fine, someone should have told you, it's not your fault but we would prefer it if you were in your normal office wear, something a bit more drab so there's more of a contrast between this world and you know. More of a 'before and after' thing.

ALICE. Oh right.

ROISIN. So sorry.

*Enter* SALLY.

SALLY. You look lovely, Alice.

ALICE. I have to change.

CAL *also appears*.

CAL. Hello, love.

*He kisses her.*

ALICE (*surprised*). Hello, you.

*She kisses him back. Much more intimacy and connection in this act.*

ROISIN. And hello there, I'm Roisin.

CAL. I'm Cal. Pleased to meet you.

ROISIN. So you're the boyfriend. Perfect.

CAL (*to* ALICE). Nice dress. Where are you going?

ALICE. I'm not allowed to wear it yet. I have to change.

CAL. Do you need a hand?

ALICE *laughs*.

*He kisses her again.*

LIZ *makes sucking, puking gestures behind his back*.

ALICE. I think I can manage, thank you.

BRIAN. Can I speak to you, Sally?

SALLY. Later.

BRIAN. Now. Did you know about this chair situation?

SALLY. Leave it, Brian.

SALLY (*to* ROISIN). Can I just have a word with you over here?

ROISIN. Of course.

*They go into the green room or office.*

Sally –

SALLY. I'm only twenty-five.

ROISIN. What?

SALLY. I'm only twenty-five.

ROISIN. Oh right.

SALLY. Which is young.

ROISIN. Really young.

SALLY. I just wanted to say that.

ROISIN. Your top is fine.

SALLY. It's not about my top. (*Beat.*) I'm only management because I have responsibilities. My dad has MS and now my mum's not well. So you know this isn't –

ROISIN. I'm so sorry.

SALLY. No. I'm not asking for you to be sorry. I just want you to know this isn't all of me, that's all.

ROISIN. Honestly, it's just a bit of context setting, that's all.

SALLY. The context being shit job, fat boss.

ROISIN. It's really only a twenty-to-thirty-second intro to Alice. It's not a big deal.

SALLY. It's the only time I'm probably going to be on TV again, though, isn't it?

ROISIN. You don't know that. Who knows?

SALLY. I do.

ROISIN. It's just a bit of fun.

SALLY. For who?

ROISIN. For everyone. Look, you guys get to have a couple of hours off, Alice gets to sing for millions of people and potentially change her life and we're going to get two minutes of TV. Everyone's happy.

SALLY. Well the couple of hours off actually costs us money because we mostly work off commission but fine.

ROISIN. Look, Sally, I work hard too. This is hard work.

SALLY. How much do you get paid though, I wonder?

ROISIN. Have I done something to upset you, Sally?

SALLY. No. (*Beat.*) No. You're just doing your job.

*Beat.*

And this is mine, I know.

### Scene Two

ROISIN *films* ALICE *and* CAL *in a couple-y pose on the sofa.*

ROISIN. That's perfect. So, Alice, who inspired you to enter the competition?

ALICE. It was actually my friend Liam who used to work here, he's gone to Colombia to work in a school. Anyway, he made me feel like it might happen, he said he thought I had something special.

ROISIN. That's perfect. Can we make it Cal, though? I'm sure he's been inspiring too.

CAL. Yeah thanks, babe.

ALICE. Oh, right.

ROISIN. Okay let's take it again.

*Beat.*

ALICE. Sorry, what, you just want me to say that all again but with Cal instead of Liam?

ROISIN. Yes and can you try and make it a full sentence and start with 'I': 'I was inspired to enter the *X-Factor* by my boyfriend Cal who blah blah blah', it's just easier to cut that way.

ALICE. That sounds a bit weird though, doesn't it? Like I'm presenting something.

ROISIN. Well you are: yourself.

ALICE. Who actually goes around saying: 'I was inspired by my boyfriend or my dying nan to become a singer and make them proud' or 'I want to build a better life for myself'. Who speaks in full sentences? Who even thinks in full sentences?

CAL. I know but this isn't real life is it, Alice? (*Gesturing around.*) This is real life.

ROISIN. Quite. How long have you worked here?

ALICE. Six months now.

CAL. More. Fuck.

ALICE. It's quite good because it's so flexible.

ROISIN. Is the money good?

ALICE. The bonuses are okay.

CAL. And if you're really lucky and have been a very good boy and sold the most they take you out to Zizzi's for a ten-quid pizza.

ROISIN. No.

CAL. Yes.

ROISIN. That's really… (*Avoids the word.*)

CAL. Patronising?

ROISIN. Exactly but I didn't want to say it you know. Didn't want to be patronising.

CAL. No it's fine. It's not us.

ALICE. I think it's quite nice.

CAL. What?

ALICE. Zizzi's.

CAL. It's alright.

ROISIN. Oh yeah Zizzi's is grand but it's not like it's really a treat is it after a while? And even the idea of a treat's a bit funny, isn't it?

*Beat.*

CAL. It's not forever and you can split your shifts up and make it fit around rehearsals.

ALICE. Cal's in a play.

CAL. It's just a little gay play but it's okay.

ALICE. You get your kit off, don't you, Cal?

CAL. Not completely.

ROISIN. Let me know where it's on. God that makes me sound like I just want to see you in the buff, doesn't it? No I like the theatre. And I know tons of agents.

ALICE. He's got an agent.

CAL. She's pissing me off.

ROISIN. God, every actor I know hates their agent.

*CAL and ROISIN laugh. ALICE does not.*

ALICE. I was inspired to enter the *X-Factor* by my boyfriend Cal who's always believed in me.

ROISIN. That's fine. How long have you guys been going out?

ALICE. A year.

ROISIN. And you guys met here?

ALICE. No we met in a pub in Camden, just down the road really.

ROISIN. Were you singing?

ALICE. No I was drinking.

ROISIN. Can we say you were singing?

CAL. Say anything you like.

ROISIN. So if you say that and just look at Cal and smile that would be great, I know it's cheesy but you two are gorgeous. We're building a bit of a narrative here.

ALICE. Is narrative another name for lying?

CAL. Yes.

ROISIN *laughs*.

ALICE *looks ill*.

ROISIN. Are you okay, Alice?

ALICE. Yeah my stomach is just a bit.

ROISIN. I always get like that when I have a drink in the day.

ALICE. I haven't –

ROISIN. Have you not? I thought I saw you and Liz coming out of the loo with a sneaky bottle of vodka. No, look I don't blame you. Dutch courage.

CAL. That's why you're so lairy.

ALICE. I had one. I'm fine.

CAL. Fuck's sake.

ROISIN. Sorry, I shouldn't have said anything. I didn't know it was a big deal.

ALICE. It's not.

CAL. No it's not.

ROISIN. Great.

ALICE (*too hard*). I just don't like being watched.

*Uncomfortable pause.*

ROISIN. Okay... I think I've got more than enough.

*Beat.*

ALICE. I'm sorry.

ROISIN. It's fine.

ALICE. No really.

ROISIN. It's cool.

ALICE. I'm just a bit nervous.

*Beat.*

I want this so much. The only thing I know how to do is sing. Oh God that's something someone would say on the *X-Factor*, isn't it? But honestly I'm shit at everything else. I'm even shit at shit jobs. I've tried gigging in bars and being in bands and it doesn't go anywhere and there's no money. This is big. This is big for me. It's all... just please don't say anything to anyone or anything. I'll say whatever you need me to say.

ROISIN. It's fine.

ALICE. Honestly, I'm sorry.

ROISIN. I really hope you do well, Alice, both of you. You're both clearly talented and deserve more than this. But honestly you know how this works. It's not really about talent, it's a lottery

ALICE. But you've got be in it to win it. Don't you?

ROISIN. Absolutely.

*Enter SALLY and the rest of the company.*

SALLY. Okay, we need to get back to work. Break is over.

*The company sit at their desks.*

ROISIN. Perfect timing. Thanks for everything, Sally.

SALLY. Fine, yes, you're welcome.

ROISIN. You were very accommodating.

BRIAN (*on the phone*). Hello, my name is Brian and I'm calling from Fame Makeover and photographic studios, is this Miss Deborah Bullock?

SALLY. I hope you got what you needed.

ROISIN. More than enough.

SALLY. I'm sure.

ROISIN*'s phone goes off.*

ROISIN. Sorry, can I just use your office?

SALLY. Why not? It's not like it's being used for anything.

ROISIN. Lovely thanks.

ROISIN *goes into the office area.*

(*On the phone.*) I know I know but these things always take forever, don't they? Usual. As you'd expect. Lots of chat. Gentle bulldozing. Super sad.

COLETTE *hovers in the doorway.*

One sec, Chris.

*Covers her phone.*

(*To* COLETTE.) Hello, gorgeous, what's up?

COLETTE. I just wondered if I could get that card.

ROISIN. Which card?

COLETTE. The one with your email. I thought maybe I could send you my video maybe see if you think there's any point in me like pursuing it.

ROISIN. Hold on one sec, Chris. (*To* COLETTE.) Which video?

COLETTE. The music video I made for my A level.

ROISIN. Oh right. Oh yeah okay. Can you just wait one second?

ROISIN *starts rooting around in the her bag while also trying to stay on her phone.*

(*To Chris on the phone.*) No it's fine keep talking… Access was always dodgy on that one. They have to be realistic. And they have to stop changing their bloody minds. I know. Totally not going to happen.

(*To* COLETTE.) Sorry, I can't find anything. Half my kitchen's in here.

(*To Chris.*) No, I'm just talking to a girl –

COLETTE. Colette.

ROISIN (*to Chris*). Fuck off. That's totally fucking not on. I'm so sorry.

COLETTE. Don't worry about it.

ROISIN (*to* COLETTE). Sorry, I can't find it and to be honest it's not really my department. There's a talent department.

COLETTE. Oh right.

ROISIN. Just send your CV in.

COLETTE. I know but I just thought it might be easier if you look at my video and then I'll know whether to bother.

ROISIN (*to Chris*). What? What? That is completely outrageous.

*She gives up rooting around in her bag and strides off to one side.*

*She wheels around. The two women look at each other.*

COLETTE. Forget it.

ROISIN. Sorry.

*Change of lighting.*

*X-Factor music.*

SALLY (*voice-over*). 'We're so proud of Alice. She's a great employee and we'd be sad to lose her but she has an amazing voice and deserves to be a star.'

*Interval.*

## ACT THREE

### Winter

*The office, night. The space is lit by half-arsed Christmas lights. Sounds of a party going on down the corridor.*

LIZ. There's nothing to you, Rob.

ROB. What do you want? Levels?

LIZ. Yes. That would be nice.

ROB. I have levels.

LIZ. Yeah?

ROB. Multiple levels. I'm multi-storey.

LIZ. A multi-storey car park maybe.

ROB. I'm a skyscraper of many levels and emotions. I'm The Shard.

LIZ. A thin pointy cock?

ROB. See unless you let me show it to you you're just going to be thinking about it non-stop, I can tell.

LIZ. Is this how your seductions normally work? You drop your pants? Just plop it out.

ROB. I do.

LIZ. And what happens? Do the girls faint?

ROB. Some do, some call the police, it's a risky strategy but you got to play big to win big, see how I keep saying big?

LIZ. Levels. I want levels.

ROB. I'll show you mine if you show me yours.

LIZ. Are you somehow implying that I don't have levels?

ROB. I'm not implying anything, I'm saying you're a dirt-bag Australian and that's all good by me.

LIZ. This must be the British charm I hear so much about.

ROB. Oh I forgot about Australia's reputation for refinement. Fucking hell, love, give us a break, it's Christmas.

LIZ. Do you know how hot it is in Queensland, right now? Don't talk to me about Christmas.

ROB. Why aren't you going home then?

*Beat.*

LIZ. You show me yours and I'll show mine.

ROB. Sob story you want, is it?

LIZ. Not necessarily. Just something that won't make me want to kill myself when I wake up with your hairy arse staring at me tomorrow morning.

ROB. What makes you think I stay the night? Spot on about the arse though.

LIZ. Robert!

ROB. Alright alright, well actually here you go: it's not Robert, my name's actually Robin.

LIZ. Like Batman and Robin?

ROB. Even worse, like The Bee Gees. The Gibbs. Robin Gibb?

LIZ. You're kidding me.

ROB. My mum was a fan.

LIZ. Why Robin? Why not the hot one with the beard?

ROB. Fuck knows.

LIZ. What does she say?

ROB. Not much. She's dead. Died when I was twelve.

LIZ. Oh dude, I'm sorry.

ROB. Yeah real shit storm. Cancer. Got to it late because she was pregnant with my sister at the time.

LIZ. Oh my God. That's horrible.

ROB. It's harder for them to detect.

*Beat.*

(*Laughing.*) Sorry, I can't. I shouldn't.

LIZ. Oh my God, are you taking the piss?

ROB. No.

ROB *laughing.*

LIZ. Was that a lie?

ROB. Yes. She's fine.

LIZ. Oh my God how can you do that?

ROB. I don't know.

LIZ. That is just fucking evil.

ROB. My dad is dead though if that helps.

LIZ. You're unreal. How can I even –

ROB (*laughing*). He is.

LIZ. – believe anything you ever?

ROB. I'm not lying. Honestly, he died when I was twelve.

LIZ. Cancer?

ROB. No. He disappeared, missing for days, everyone worried he'd been murdered or shacked up with someone else, all of that, turns out he hung himself in a forest, didn't he, the stupid twat.

*Beat.*

LIZ. Is that for real?

ROB. Yeah.

*Beat.*

LIZ. You shouldn't joke about death.

ROB. Nah you should always joke about death. I mean what else can you do.

*Pause.*

LIZ. And is your name really Robin?

ROB. Yes.

LIZ. Honestly?

ROB. Honestly? No.

LIZ. You're so full of shit.

ROB. Yeah. Yeah I am.

LIZ. That is so irritating. That glib acceptance. I am what I am I can't possibly change or grow as a human being. You should be ashamed. Why aren't you ashamed?

ROB. Ashamed of what?

LIZ. Well putting aside your mum's fake cancerous womb, which I'm not sure I can, there's being totally okay with conning old women into buy shitty photographic makeovers. Being a prick to Brian. Hitting on every woman with a pulse and generally being a ruthless, capitalist, self-serving cunt.

*Beat.*

ROB. So how did the interview go? Are you going to be my boss?

*Beat.*

LIZ. Fuck.

ROB. Busted. Everyone knows.

LIZ. I don't know. It went well. I can string words of more than one syllable together, which helped. If it's between me and Brian then I'll probably get it. Why didn't you apply?

ROB. Sally's not my number-one fan. Things are moving though. Things are falling into place. I'm just one step away from a serious sales job, somewhere legit.

LIZ. I don't know if I'll take it.

ROB. But you applied. You applied for Sally's job? You applied to run an elite squad who specialise in conning old women into buying shitty photographic makeovers.

LIZ. Look, I was in a really vulnerable place when I did the application. I'd just broken up with Horst, I'd had a heavy weekend, it was a Sunday evening there was a Richard Curtis movie on ITV2.

ROB. You don't have to apologise.

LIZ. I'm not. I'm explaining.

ROB. You don't need to explain. I get it. You're full of shit too. That's alright.

LIZ. Is it?

ROB. Listen.

*Moving towards her.*

I think you're lovely looking, I think you're the funniest, weirdest, hottest, prettiest dirt-bag I've ever met and I would like to kiss you because it's Christmas and this party is fucking awful and because I like you.

*Beat.*

LIZ. Let's do it then.

ROB. Really?

LIZ. Why not?

ROB. You're the boss.

LIZ. Do you have any coke?

ROB. No.

LIZ. Yes you do.

ROB. I've got some MDMA.

LIZ. Fucking A.

ROB *gets out an envelope.*

ROB (*as he dabs a bit in his mouth*). Dib for me.

LIZ. Dib dib dab for me.

*She scoops out loads and puts in her mouth.*

ROB. You are not a cheap date.

ROB *looks around. He kisses her.*

LIZ. Not bad.

ROB. Yeah?

LIZ. Yeah.

ROB. You're alright.

LIZ. I'm better than alright. I'm going to blow your tiny mind.

*She kisses him and grabs his crotch.*

Let's see your other level then.

ROB. You for real?

LIZ. Just get it out.

ROB. What if someone comes in?

LIZ. Everyone's on the roof.

ROB. But there's people passing.

LIZ. That's what makes it fun, isn't it? Come on, you dirty bitch.

ROB. Ruthless cunt.

*They kiss. She feels his crotch.*

LIZ. Promising.

*He turns his back to the audience and pulls out his cock to show* LIZ.

I can't see it.

ROB. Shut the fuck up.

LIZ. No I mean I can't see. Undo your shirt.

ROB. Oh. Okay.

*He undoes his shirt.*

LIZ. That'll do.

*She kisses him some more, rubs up against him.*

ROB. It will more than just do. Just give us a minute.

*She rubs him some more.*

*The moment goes on a bit long.*

*She goes down on him.*

*Sound of the party upstairs, music from somewhere.*

*She stops, leans back.*

LIZ. Are you okay?

ROB. Keep going.

LIZ. You like your balls pulled?

ROB. Yeah.

LIZ. You like that?

ROB. Yeah.

LIZ. Yeah slap me with it. That's it. Slap my face.

*We can see from behind, him slapping her face with his dick.*

*She moans.*

*He tries to fluff himself.*

ROB. Sorry, I'm never normally. Out like a shot normally.

*He keeps fluffing himself then stops.*

LIZ. Keep going.

ROB. Sorry, it's not really happening.

*He starts to do himself up.*

LIZ. Is that it?

ROB. Yeah. Maybe. Sorry.

*LIZ starts laughing.*

That doesn't help get me up, okay.

*The laughter becomes something more racked and desperate.*

Hey I'm sorry. Don't take it personally. I'm just too pissed. Let's do it another time.

*Silence.*

Are you alright?

LIZ. I'm just a bit tired. Bit emosh. I feel like I haven't slept in eight years. I haven't had my own room since I was eighteen, it's always a dorm, or someone's sofa or someone's sublet or this life-changing commune in a wooden hut in Bali and it's all been fucking amazing. Just totally, totally, enriching. Really really fun.

*Silence.*

*Voices offstage coming closer.*

Fuck. Fuck.

*They reach around for their clothes and do themselves up.*

ROB. Shit.

LIZ. Fuck.

*They exit as* ALICE *and* CAL *enter from the other entrance.*

ALICE. And this was the one you'd given up on? The one where you were convinced the casting director hated you?

CAL. She did.

ALICE. She obviously didn't. She obviously loved you. Fancied you probably. This is the Weinstein one, right?

CAL. Yeah.

ALICE. Oh my God. That's a big deal. This is. I'm so happy for you. Are you happy?

CAL.

ALICE. Be happy, Cal.

CAL. I am.

ALICE. Well try and look less like someone murdered your whole family then.

CAL. You're happy though?

ALICE. Of course I'm happy. I'm happy for you. What are you worried about?

CAL. I don't want to make it into a big deal.

ALICE. Why not? It is a big deal. Let yourself enjoy it.

CAL. I am.

*Beat.*

ALICE. I mean it's probably going to be a disaster.

CAL. It probably is.

ALICE. It's probably going to be a flop.

CAL. It could be.

ALICE. And all the critics and the Weinsteins will personally blame you and you will never be cast in anything again, I mean I expect that's what's going to happen.

CAL (*laughing*). I expect so.

*Beat.*

Come here.

ALICE. You will never work in this town again.

CAL. You're the best.

ALICE. You're the worst. The worst actor in the history of film.

CAL. Alright, alright. Enough of that.

*He grabs her and kisses her.*

ALICE. Oh my God, you're going to be in a bloody Weinstein movie.

*She does a little scream.*

CAL. Shhhh.

ALICE. Let's get hammered.

CAL. No, let's not.

ALICE. We're celebrating.

CAL. Just take it easy, yeah. You promised.

ALICE. Yeah alright. Hey in America they'd think I were proper wild, wouldn't they? They don't really drink in Hollywood, do they? They just eat kale and meditate. Is that going to be you? Are you going to buff up and become a superhero? Are you going to become a Scientologist? Or a drug addict. Or hate Jews. God, everyone's going to think you're gay.

CAL. Why are they going to think that?

ALICE. Because you're pretty. Fucking hell. This is huge.

CAL. You're happy.

ALICE. Of course I'm bloody happy.

CAL. I wasn't sure if you were going to be happy.

ALICE. Why wouldn't I be happy?

CAL. Because I'm going to move there, Alice.

ALICE. To Hollywood?

CAL. That was always the plan.

ALICE. I know but –

CAL. You didn't think it was going to happen? Thanks.

ALICE. No, but sometimes things change, don't they?

CAL. Only if you let them.

ALICE. Or they don't work out and it's not your fault.

CAL. It's always been the plan.

ALICE. For how long?

CAL. I don't know.

ALICE. But you'll come back and forth.

CAL. Probably not that much.

*Beat.*

ALICE. Well I'll come out. I'll move.

CAL.

ALICE. Unless you don't want me to.

CAL. I'd love you to visit. Come for a holiday.

ALICE. But not stay?

CAL.

ALICE. What's happening, Cal?

CAL. I just don't think it makes sense to do the long-distance thing. I'm sorry.

ALICE. I said I'd move.

CAL. What would you do?

ALICE. I don't know, work.

CAL. As what?

ALICE. Bar, call centre, teach, I don't mind.

CAL. You'll need a visa.

ALICE. I'll apply.

CAL. They're really strict.

ALICE. Movie stars only?

CAL. Something like that.

ALICE. Well I'm sorry I'm not a movie star.

CAL. I can't deal with this.

ALICE. Deal with what?

CAL. Sorry, that's bad of me. This isn't your fault. The thing is I'm just going to really need to focus on myself when I'm out there. I know that sounds selfish but I can't look after anyone else, I can't carry anyone else.

ALICE. I'm not asking you to carry me. I just love you, don't I?

CAL. I knew you'd be like this. This is what I mean. You're just not able to give me the support I'm going to need.

*Beat.*

ALICE. I give you loads of support.

CAL. I need a different kind of support now. Everything's changed. It's actually really scary. Really exposing.

ALICE. Is it?

CAL. You just don't get it and that's fine.

*Beat.*

ALICE. Does Roisin get it?

CAL. Okay, this is all getting a bit unnecessary now, isn't it?

ALICE. Your new agent's a friend of hers, right? They're all friends. Roisin and what's your agent called?

CAL. Fi.

ALICE. Fi. Of course. Fi and Roisin understand how it all works. Roisin could probably give you the new support you need, couldn't she?

CAL. Honestly this is really petty.

ALICE. Maybe I am petty. Maybe I'm small. Maybe I'm nothing. Just say I'm not good enough.

CAL. No.

ALICE. Just say I'm a failure. That's what you're thinking.

CAL. I'm not thinking that.

ALICE. I'm just going to drag you down with my mediocrity? You've been different ever since the *X-Factor*.

CAL. I'm not listening now.

ALICE. It's not infectious. You won't catch failure.

*She reaches out to try and touch him.*

*He shrinks away.*

Or maybe it is.

CAL. Are you drunk?

ALICE. No. You know / I'm not.

CAL. You drink too much.

ALICE. Shut up.

CAL. It's not right. Something's not right about it. I'm actually worried about you.

ALICE. Yeah you seem really worried.

CAL. You don't want to end up like Liz.

ALICE. What's wrong with Liz?

CAL. She's a mess.

ALICE. She's my friend.

CAL. How old is she?

ALICE. Twenty-four, twenty-five.

CAL. She's a fuck-up. She's a mess. And she's a drunk and now she's going to end up running this place. If I'm anywhere near a place like this at twenty-five shoot me.

ALICE *catches sight of something offstage.*

ALICE. Liam?

LIAM *enters*.

LIAM. Hi.

ALICE. What are you doing here?

LIAM. Rob invited me.

ALICE. No I mean here. Why aren't you in Colombia?

CAL. You saved the world already?

LIAM. Yeah all done.

CAL. Good work.

LIAM. You alright?

CAL. Yeah we're fine.

*Beat.*

ALICE. Liam?

LIAM. What?

ALICE. You're not back, are you?

LIAM. I'm just going to have a chat with Sally.

CAL. Cool. We'll get out of your way. Let's go, Alice.

ALICE. Oh fuck off, Cal.

*Beat.*

CAL. She's all yours, mate.

CAL *exits*.

ALICE *stands watching* LIAM.

LIAM. Everything alright?

ALICE.

*The moment holds.*

SALLY *enters*.

SALLY. Sorry for the wait, Liam, I'm just bringing Duncan in. Hi, Alice. Merry Christmas.

ALICE. Merry Christmas.

*ALICE exits.*

*Beat.*

SALLY. So you're back.

LIAM. That I am.

SALLY. Early.

LIAM. Yes.

SALLY. No tan?

LIAM. Sunstroke peels right off.

SALLY. Ouch.

LIAM. My fault. My kind weren't ever really meant to leave the Donegal.

SALLY. How was it?

LIAM (*deadpan*). Life-changing, yeah.

SALLY. How was the school?

LIAM. The kids were great. Not sure I was up to much as a teacher.

SALLY. Did they run riot?

LIAM. No. Well, there were two little fuckers called Elvis and Jesus but no it wasn't that. It was hard. Proper. Really hard out there and what the fuck do I know about anything?

SALLY. And the people you were with?

LIAM. The other foreigners? Just like here. We got pissed a lot. Might as well have been here.

SALLY. And so you came back?

LIAM. It wasn't for me.

SALLY. What is for you?

*Enter DUNCAN.*

DUNCAN. Sorry, I got stuck with Brian. Great guy.

SALLY. No worries. Do you remember Liam?

DUNCAN (*he doesn't*). Of course. Totally. How's it going?

LIAM. Yeah good thanks. I just got back from Colombia.

DUNCAN. Fucking hell, I love Colombia. Did you go to Bogata?

LIAM. Yes.

DUNCAN. Did you go to Harry's Bar?

LIAM. No. I heard about it.

DUNCAN (*for* SALLY*'s benefit*). It's this cool cocktail bar, totally weird; it's like Mayfair or Madison Avenue or something in the middle of this totally shit hole neighbourhood. Amazing martinis and steaks. It's amazing. It's an amazing country. Gets a really bad rap.

LIAM. Yeah I worked in a school up in –

DUNCAN (*not listening*). Amazing place. Travelling?

LIAM. Volunteering.

DUNCAN. Oh yeah. One of those.

*Beat.*

Did your heart bleed?

LIAM (*not backing down*). It did.

DUNCAN. Right.

LIAM. Not so much the poverty, no one had much but they got on with things. It was the violence. Women just beaten as if it's nothing. Kids with guns. Not like water pistols. Real guns.

DUNCAN. Right.

*Beat.*

SALLY. I was going to offer Liam some shifts but obviously because I'm going and we haven't announced anything yet, I just thought I'd get your sign-off. Liam was our top seller.

*Beat.*

DUNCAN. Were you now?

LIAM. Yeah I think so.

DUNCAN. So what's the plan then?

LIAM. Stop kipping on Rob's floor but I need to save up for a deposit first.

DUNCAN. And then what?

LIAM. Maybe an MA.

DUNCAN. What for?

LIAM. You need an MA.

DUNCAN. Do you?

LIAM. You do in international relations.

DUNCAN. You don't need an MA to sell. You don't even need a degree. What are fees now? Nine grand a year plus living costs? That's practically a deposit. You could have bought a house by now.

LIAM. Not in London.

DUNCAN. Don't buy in London then.

LIAM. But I live in London.

DUNCAN. You don't have to live in the house. It's an investment. Look…

LIAM. Liam.

DUNCAN. Liam. I was eighteen when I left school. Within a year I was a supervisor, not here, another place, proper cold-calling, brutal stuff but serious commission money. Saved. Work. Promoted. Two-bed flat in Hull by the time I was twenty-one which I rent out to students, a flat in Dartford and now I'm an area supervisor here with no debts, capital and disposable cash so I can go to Harry's Bar in Colombia and spend money which is what they actually need, right? Money. Alright alright, they need more than that but what they don't need is for you to babysit their kids and feel bad about yourself, do they?

LIAM. Probably not.

DUNCAN. And what was the point of making yourself bankrupt in the process?

LIAM. None really.

SALLY. Life experience.

DUNCAN. What's your five-year plan?

LIAM.

DUNCAN. Two-year plan?

LIAM. I don't know what I'm doing tomorrow. It's hard to imagine tomorrow.

DUNCAN. Rubbish. Tomorrow will just be like today but if you play it right you'll be richer. If you play it wrong you won't. Actually that's not quite right, the future will be like today but harder so you have to work harder, sell harder, be harder.

LIAM. Are you coming on to me, Duncan?

*Beat.*

*Nervous glances traded between* SALLY *and* LIAM.

DUNCAN *laughs. The tension is released.*

DUNCAN. Sorry, mate, not my type.

LIAM. No that's pretty much the consensus around here.

SALLY. Cal gave his notice so there will be more shifts.

DUNCAN. If we rehire. Sales have been dropping. (*To* LIAM.) Do you think we'll need to rehire or could you handle more calls if we increased the hours? Don't worry about your job for a minute.

*Beat.*

LIAM. Maybe, we probably could if we had to.

DUNCAN. If we hire you, are you going to fuck off again?

LIAM. Look, Duncan, to be honest this has always just been a money job for me.

DUNCAN. Money job. I love that. What does that even mean? That's all jobs are. Really though?

*Enter the rest of the company with a cake and presents.*

SALLY. Oh God. Is this for me?

LIZ. Too right.

ROB. We're going to miss you, Sally.

SALLY. You're not.

ROB. No we're not.

*Laughter.*

Brian is. Brian was crying earlier.

LIZ. Don't be a dick.

BRIAN. I just want to say a few words.

DUNCAN. Great. So I just want to say a few words.

SALLY. Really we don't have to do this.

DUNCAN. Of course we do. Right. So... Sally. Wow. It's been a pleasure. You've been with us, what? Two years?

SALLY. Five.

DUNCAN. Before my time.

SALLY. Yes.

DUNCAN. But two as manager.

SALLY. Longer.

DUNCAN. Ha. That's me told.

*Laughter.*

What can you say about Sally? No seriously, what can you say? I'm joking. There's lots to say. She's tough. No, she is firm but fair. She took her responsibilities seriously and

Worked hard and I wish her every luck in all her new
endeavours.

*Beat.*

That's it. To Sally.

ALL. To Sally.

*They sip from their drinks.*

SALLY. Thank you.

DUNCAN. Let's all get drunk.

ROB. Whoop whoop.

COLETTE. We got a couple of things for you.

SALLY. That's very kind.

COLETTE. It's not much.

SALLY. It's more than I expected, honestly.

*She opens up a gift. It's bath salts.*

*Everyone is underwhelmed.*

Bath salts!

BRIAN. Now you won't smell.

ROB. Good one, Brian.

SALLY. Very thoughtful.

*Beat.*

LIZ. Who the fuck chose the gift?

SALLY. No it's great. So, I've written some things down in case
this happened.

BRIAN. I want to say a few words.

*Throughout her speech the other characters whisper among
themselves.*

SALLY. It's fine. I just wanted to say. Best look at the cards.
(*Beat.*) So surprisingly to me and probably everyone else it's

been a lot more emotional than I thought it would be to say goodbye to this place and to you all. / I've learnt a huge amount about leadership. It may sound like a cop-out but it's not easy being the boss, there is a lot I would have handled differently. I think what Duncan means when he says was tough is that I was stressed and I've learnt a lot about how to deal with stress as my priorities changed –

LIZ (*to* ALICE, *under her breath*). Are you okay?

ALICE. Cal dumped me.

LIZ. What the fuck. (*To* SALLY) Sorry. (*To* ALICE.) Are you shitting me? Where is he? I'm going to fucking deck him.

ROB. What's going on?

BRIAN. Shush.

ALICE. Rob, is Liam back?

BRIAN. I want to say something.

DUNCAN. Pass us the champagne, love.

LIZ. Hang on a minute, dude.

BRIAN. Can I say something yet?

COLETTE. Let Sally speak, Brian.

BRIAN. Sorry, Sally.

COLETTE. Carry on, Sally.

SALLY. No it's fine. It sounds like you're talking about something really important. What's happened? Has Cal dumped Alice?

*Beat.*

Look I know it's a shitty job and I know you're all terribly worried about your shitty lives but if you could just…

Fuck it. Fuck it. Tonight is my first night off in a year. In a month's time I'm going to become a full-time carer for my parents. That's my new endeavour, Duncan, which I definitely told you about by the way.

DUNCAN. Sally, maybe we –

SALLY. Caring sounds nice. Caring sounds caring, doesn't it?
It doesn't sound like work but it is because caring mostly
involves cleaning the shit out of my dad's bum. It means
holding my crying mum because she's scared of dying and
having to say it's alright. It's going to be alright when I have
no bloody idea what that means. That's work. This is all just…

*Beat.*

Fuck you all and have a merry merry Christmas.

*Silence.*

LIZ. Sal?

SALLY. Yes.

LIZ. Do you want to drink?

SALLY. Yes.

LIZ. Do you want to dance?

SALLY. Yes.

LIZ. Do you want some MDMA?

SALLY. YES!

LIZ. Let's go to the roof.

DUNCAN. I'm not hearing any of this. Take me to the roof.

BRIAN. To the roof. Wait. Was there something I wanted to say?

ROB. No.

*Loud music as they exit.*

*ALICE and LIAM are left alone.*

LIAM. Are you okay?

ALICE. I'm fine.

LIAM. What's happened with Cal then?

ALICE.

LIAM. He's a knob.

ALICE. I know.

LIAM. You deserve better.

ALICE. It doesn't matter. It honestly doesn't fucking matter, does it? Did you hear about *X-Factor*?

LIAM. No.

ALICE. I went on *X-Factor*. I got through the first five auditions, which they do before they even put a camera on you and I made it to the live audition stage.

LIAM. Wow.

*Beat.*

ALICE. You heard.

LIAM.

ALICE. Rob would have said. Did he say?

LIAM. Yeah.

ALICE. Have you seen the clip?

LIAM. Yeah. You were great.

ALICE. You don't have to say that.

LIAM. I'm not.

*Beat.*

ALICE. Still whatever doesn't kill you makes you stronger or whatever that Cheryl Cole Fernandez whatever (anorexic bint) says and who fucking cares, right?

LIAM. I care.

ALICE. Do you?

LIAM. You know I do.

ALICE. Yeah I know. I don't know why though. I'm boring. I'm average.

LIAM. You're not.

ALICE. Louis Walsh said it so it must be true.

LIAM. As if Louis Walsh has said anything interesting in his life.

ALICE. They all said I was boring.

LIAM. It was the song.

ALICE. It was not the song.

LIAM. Just nerves.

ALICE. I was nervous.

LIAM. You could tell.

ALICE. I fucked up.

LIAM. No, you were great.

*Beat.*

ALICE. I wasn't.

LIAM. I think you're great.

ALICE. I know. But you're full of shit, aren't you, Liam?

LIAM. Why? What have I done wrong?

ALICE. You've come back.

LIAM *is left on his own. He swigs from his beer. We hear snatches of a song.*

*Suddenly the music cuts out.*

*Sound of screams and shouts upstairs.*

BRIAN *appears, drained of colour.*

LIAM. Brian?

*He stands frozen.*

SALLY *enters followed by* COLLETE.

SALLY. Everyone just stay in here till they come.

LIAM. What's happened?

DUNCAN *enters phone in hand.*

DUNCAN. They're on their way. They'll be here soon. I should go down.

SALLY. I'll go too.

DUNCAN. No, everyone stays here till they come.

LIAM. What's happened?

SALLY. She fell.

LIAM. Who?

COLETTE. She was dancing on the ledge.

LIAM. Who fell?

*Blackout.*

## ACT FOUR

*End of January. One month later. The office.*

ROB (*on the phone*). It's just a fancy word for hairdresser, Mrs Harris, and make-up's just a bit of slap that's right. Don't worry we have lots of slap.

COLETTE *enters*.

BRIAN. Where have you been?

COLETTE. I told Liam I was coming in late.

BRIAN. No one told me.

COLETTE. Sorry, Bri.

BRIAN. I tried calling you.

COLETTE. My phone must have been off. Where's Alice?

BRIAN. That's what I was calling about.

COLETTE. What's happened? She okay?

BRIAN. She just keeps stopping.

COLETTE. Did she say what was wrong?

BRIAN. No.

COLETTE. Did you ask her?

BRIAN.

COLETTE. Very helpful, Brian.

BRIAN. I'm not very good at 'lady things'.

ROB *laughs*.

ROB. No, Mrs Harris, I wasn't laughing at you. / Times are tough. I know, my credit card knows but this is a great deal and more than that, it's a treat and what's wrong with a treat now and then? Exactly! Otherwise what's the point of being alive?

COLETTE. Everyone needs to help with Alice. I can't be here all the time.

BRIAN. I didn't know what to do.

COLETTE (*softening*). It's okay. Has anyone noticed yet?

BRIAN. Not yet.

COLETTE *heads towards the green room.*

COLETTE *enters the green room.*

ALICE *is on the sofa, curled up under her coat.*

COLETTE (*call and response*). Alright, babez.

ALICE. Yes, babez.

COLETTE. Feel sick?

ALICE *nods, curls up to* COLETTE.

ALICE. I'm cold.

COLETTE. Do you want to go home?

ALICE. I'm fine. Just want to sleep.

COLETTE. I can take you home.

ALICE. I don't want to move.

COLETTE. We can get a taxi.

ALICE. You smell nice.

COLETTE. You'd be more comfortable at home.

ALICE. I don't want to be on my own. Could you stay with me?

COLETTE. I've only just got in.

ALICE. Where were you?

COLETTE. It doesn't matter.

ALICE. Let's just stay like this then.

COLETTE. Okay. For a bit.

ALICE. Forever.

COLETTE. For a bit.

ALICE *snuggles up against* COLETTE.

ALICE. Hey, are you coming to the pub tonight?

COLETTE. I don't know.

ALICE. You have to.

COLETTE. I've got to study.

ALICE. Please. You can stay at mine, it's fine.

COLETTE. Rob might have something to say about that.

ALICE. Rob's alright.

COLETTE. Just lie down here for a bit, love. There's nothing to worry about you're just ill and tired and sad. We all are.

*Enter* ROB *with* BRIAN.

ROB. Rise and shine, sleepy heads. The funeral's over.

COLETTE. We're trying to have a bit of quiet time, Rob.

ALICE. No it's alright. You alright?

ROB. I'm alright. (*To* COLETTE.) Did you hear what happened earlier?

COLETTE. No.

ALICE. This is good.

ROB. He gave me a bollocking about reading the paper.

COLETTE. Why would he do that?

ROB. Well I was on a call but like that fucking matters. Apparently it's a new policy. It's a brave new world, kids.

COLETTE. Be nice. He's just trying to do his job.

ROB. Shove over.

*He sits next to* ALICE *and puts his arm around her.*
COLETTE *gets out of the way.*

Feeling better, misery guts?

*He squeezes* ALICE*'s midriff.*

ALICE. Don't do that!

COLETTE. Careful, Rob.

ALICE. What you doing?

ROB. Squeezing your muffin top.

ALICE. Fuck off. I don't have a muffin top, do I?

ROB. Course you do. And I love it.

ALICE. Stop.

ROB. Never. It's so juicy, and delicious. I want to eat it all.

COLETTE (*with authority*). Rob, stop. Alice isn't feeling well.

ROB. Are you alright?

ALICE. Just a bit of a dodgy stomach. I'm fine.

ROB. The shits, is it?

ALICE *can't help laughing.*

Shit yourself, did you?

ALICE. No.

ROB *grabs her. They giggle and squirm around each other
as* LIAM *enters.*

*They stop.*

LIAM. Bit early for a break, isn't it?

ALICE. I wasn't feeling well.

LIAM. What's wrong? Do you need to go home?

ALICE. No, I'm fine now.

ROB. I've cured her. I have the magic touch.

*He licks his fingers.*

LIAM. Is that your paper on the desk, Rob?

ROB. Don't know.

LIAM. Just get rid of it, yeah, before Duncan sees?

ROB. Duncan, is it?

LIAM. Yeah it is.

ALICE. Can we really not read the papers any more, Liam?

LIAM. No.

ALICE. What even the *Metro*?

LIAM. Look I know it's annoying but I'm also trying to make some good changes. Did you get my email?

ROB. Which one?

LIAM. The one flagged urgent.

ROB. Nope.

LIAM. Did everyone else get it?

COLETTE. I haven't been in this morning.

LIAM. It's marked Changes (Data Entry).

ROB. Great title. When's the movie coming out?

ALICE *laughs*.

LIAM. No I think you'll like it. It means less work for everyone. It's actually really interesting being this side of it. I can really see how we can do things better. It's actually quite cool.

ROB. Yeah you seem really cool right now.

COLETTE. What's the idea?

LIAM. In some ways it's quite simple but in other ways it's actually quite radical. So you know that bit after the sale

when for some unknown reason you have to log it again
even though the sale is automatically logged?

ALICE. Not really.

LIAM. No you do, we used to moan about it all the time?…
Well we're not going to do that any more. It was just
duplication.

COLETTE. That's a good idea.

LIAM. Thanks.

BRIAN. If you ask me, this is just asking for trouble.

LIAM. In what way?

BRIAN. If it's not broke.

LIAM. It's not necessarily broke but it could be better.

BRIAN. Change for change sake.

LIAM. Do you have a problem with this arrangement, Brian? /
I'm sorry you didn't get the job but –

COLETTE. I think you guys should talk about this in your
office.

BRIAN. I just don't see any point upsetting the apple cart.
Throwing babies out with bath water.

LIAM. There's going to be quite big changes coming and
you're going to need to be a bit more flexible.

ALICE. What kind of changes?

COLETTE. I really think you guys should talk about this in
private.

ALICE. No, tell us what's happening.

LIAM. Well it's going to be a smaller team. Fewer people
working full-time hours, probably more freelancers but a
smaller core. More flexibility in some ways which is good.

BRIAN. Tightening the belt.

LIAM. That's right.

BRIAN. Sacrifices.

LIAM. Some.

BRIAN. Just as well Liz died then, isn't it?

ALICE. What the fuck?

*Beat.*

Was that a joke?

BRIAN. No. Was it funny?

ALICE. No it fucking wasn't.

ROB. What's wrong with your head, Bri.

BRIAN. I don't understand.

ROB *pushes at* BRIAN.

COLETTE. Stay calm, we're all in shock.

BRIAN. Well you can't just spring this on people in a memo. It's going to completely change the way we deal with calls.

COLETTE. I meant Liz.

BRIAN. Oh I see. (*Beat*.) But that's it. People come and go, they always do. That's why you need a clear system so everyone knows where they are. If you start changing things, if you start messing around with the order then no one knows where they are and then how do you know where anything is, how do you know up is up or down is down or where you are or who you are. It's just a mess. A disgusting, disgusting mess. And I don't. And I don't. And I don't. I want everything as it was please. Now. Thank you.

*He exits into the work area.*

ROB. Back to work then, is it, boss man?

LIAM. Don't be like that, Rob. You know how it is.

ROB. I don't as it goes.

*He exits into the space, followed by* ALICE.

LIAM *sags*.

LIAM. Why are they being like this?

COLETTE. Maybe just give them a bit of time to get used to it. It's funny they remind me of my baby nieces when they fall over and they're stunned; they can't work out what happened. Like 'I was cool, I was running around and now I'm on the floor and I'm in pain and it's all your fault.'

LIAM. Exactly.

COLETTE. They're all upside down at the moment. Rob's angry, Alice is sad but she can't stay still and Brian's. Well he's finding it hard. It's up to you but I'd leave it a bit before you change things too much.

LIAM. Okay, I'll lay off the changes for a bit.

COLETTE. Only if you think it's a good idea.

LIAM. You know if Brian ever went…

COLETTE. I don't know what I'm doing yet.

LIAM. How did it go?

COLETTE. It was good. It was great actually. They offered it to me.

LIAM. Right.

COLETTE. But I haven't said yes yet.

LIAM. Why not?

COLETTE. There is some money but it's less than here. It's basically an internship.

LIAM. But at the BBC.

COLETTE. At the BBC.

LIAM. Your parents would understand that, won't they?

COLETTE. They worry. I better get on. Thanks for being cool about this morning and the reference.

LIAM. Of course.

*They enter the work space.*

Well done, guys. Have a great day.

ROB. Thanks, boss.

LIAM *exits in one direction.*

ROB *makes a gesture behind his back.*

COLETTE. Where's Alice now?

ROB. Toilet.

COLETTE. You need to keep an eye on her.

ROB. She seems fine now.

COLETTE. She isn't.

ROB. She'll be alright.

COLETTE. You two need to calm it.

ROB. Calm what?

COLETTE. Going out. The drinking.

ROB. What else are we supposed to do?

COLETTE. I don't know but you can't keep it up.

ROB. Is that a challenge?

COLETTE. I'm being serious, Rob.

ROB. I know and it's fucking boring.

*Enter* ALICE.

ALICE. What's going on?

ROB. Apparently we need to cool the drinking, Alice.

ALICE. Who said that?

ROB. Colette.

COLETTE. It wasn't like that. I just think we all need to look after each other.

ALICE. Well come out for a drink more often. It's fun when we all go out.

COLETTE. I can't do it every night. I just can't.

ALICE. We've got to develop your stamina.

COLETTE. It's more the next day. I feel so sad in the mornings.

*Beat.*

ALICE. You believe in God, don't you, Colette?

ROB. Fucking hell.

COLETTE. Let's not talk about that.

ALICE. Why not?

COLETTE. Because you all take the piss.

ALICE. I'm not taking the piss. I want to know. I want to know what it's like.

COLETTE. It's too hard to explain.

ALICE. I wish I believed in God.

ROB. The biggest get-out-of-jail-free card.

COLETTE. It's not. It doesn't work like that. Faith is really hard. Well it is for me anyway. It's different for my mum but it's something I have to really work at.

*Silence.*

BRIAN. Pay day.

ROB. Thank the Lord.

COLETTE (*laughing off the seriousness*). Amen.

ALICE. It's just going to be base for me. I don't think I've made a sale in weeks.

COLETTE. That's understandable.

ALICE. Too fucking right it is.

BRIAN *hands out the payslips, saying their names as he does so.*

BRIAN. Robert Gibson, Alice Nutter, Colette D'Silva, Caleb Love.

*Beat.*

(*To* ALICE.) Will you be seeing Cal? Could you pass it along?

ALICE. No I will not be seeing Cal as it goes, Bri.

COLETTE. Let's just make it through the day, guys. (*Referring to his pile of envelopes*.) Is Liz's there?

BRIAN. Uhm, yes, yes it is.

COLETTE. I'll send it to Sandra.

ALICE. How is her mum?

COLETTE. Not great.

ALICE. I meant to Skype. I was going to Skype every Sunday. I haven't done it once yet.

COLETTE. She'd understand.

ALICE. I don't.

COLETTE. We should get on.

*She settles down and looks at her phone.*

(*On the phone*.) Hello, can I speak to Ms Madekwe? No that's okay, maybe I can talk to you until she's back.

*She opens her payslip as she talks.*

What's your name, hon? Joy? That's a pretty name. How old are you, Joy?

BRIAN (*on the phone*). And how are you this wintry afternoon, Mrs Parsons?

ALICE *looks around at the office.*

COLETTE. What magazines do you like? No I don't read them much but I like the pictures. Do you like pictures of models, honey?

COLETTE *looks alarmed by the payslip.*

ROB (*on the phone*). Is that Mr Coates. Is the lady of the house in?

*ALICE can't face it and she exits back to the green room, puts the blanket back around herself. After a while we see her drinking from a hip flask.*

BRIAN. And goodbye, Mrs Parsons.

ROB (*on the phone to the aggressive Mr Coates*). I will certainly do that. I will stick it right up there.

Cunt.

COLETTE (*on the phone*). One second, honey, keep talking.

*She hands over her payslip to* ROB.

ROB. What?

COLETTE (*whispering*). Look at the last line. (*On the phone.*) Would you like some photographs of you and your family, do you think?

ROB. What the fuck?

BRIAN. What's going on?

ROB. Fucking hell.

*He opens his own payslip.*

It's on mine too.

COLETTE. Sorry, Joy, I'm going to have to call you back.

ROB (*referring to the payslip*). They're having a joke.

COLETTE. This must be a mistake.

ROB. A sick, fucking joke.

COLETTE. They wouldn't do that, would they?

ROB. They fucking would.

BRIAN. Is there something wrong?

ROB. Yes, Brian. There's something very wrong. Do you know about this?

BRIAN. Know about what?

ROB. The fucking deduction.

*He hands him his payslip.*

BRIAN. Ah. Right-o. I see.

ROB. Do you? Do you fucking see? Would you like to see my
fist in your face, mate?

COLETTE. Is it a mistake?

BRIAN. I don't know.

COLETTE. It must be.

*Enter* ALICE.

ROB. Does Liam know about this? (*To* BRIAN.) Did you know
about it?

ALICE. Know about what?

*Silence.*

COLETTE. They're not paying us basic for the day we went to
Liz's service.

*Beat.*

But I think it's a mistake. Someone in finance must have just
added up the hours but forgot about it or didn't know.

ROB. Finance is two people. They knew. And anyway someone
has to sign off on it, don't they? Have you signed off on this,
geektard?

BRIAN. Of course not.

ALICE. Where's Liam?

BRIAN. He's in his office.

ROB. This is outrageous. This is fucking. She fucking fell from
this fucking roof. This fucking building. This fucking place.
We watched. We watched. Motherfuckers.

*He kicks something.*

COLETTE. Stop shouting, you're upsetting Brian.

ROB. Am I, mate? Are you upset, mate?

ALICE. Where's Liam?

BRIAN. I didn't know.

COLETTE. Keep calm, Rob.

BRIAN. I didn't know.

ALICE. Liam!

COLETTE. I know. It's not Brian's fault.

ROB. How do we know? He's management.

COLETTE. Come on, it's Brian, he wouldn't do this.

ALICE (*screaming*). Liam. LIAM!

  LIAM *appears*.

  (*Holding up the payslip*.) Did you know about this?

LIAM. Are you okay, Alice?

ALICE. No. No, I'm not, Liam, as it goes.

LIAM. What's going on?

  *Beat*.

ROB. Mate, they're docking us for Liz's funeral.

LIAM.

  *Beat*.

ALICE. Liam?

LIAM. Can I see?

  *He takes the payslip*.

COLETTE. It's a mistake, right?

LIAM. No, not technically. They've added up the hours correctly.

ALICE. But they can't be serious about this, can they? They're not going to dock us the hours.

LIAM. The problem is we didn't work. They don't have to pay us for time we haven't worked. It's like sick pay.

ALICE. But this is different. It happened here.

LIAM. I know but they're not responsible.

ALICE. Who's responsible?

LIAM. They don't owe us; they don't legally need to give us time off.

ALICE. But that's not the point.

LIAM. They should.

COLETTE. Of course they should. Look, do they know that's where we were on that day? Maybe it's –

LIAM. It's a blanket policy. You get paid for what you work but I agree it's insensitive.

COLETTE. So it's not a mistake?

ROB. Keep up, love.

COLETTE. I just don't understand how anyone could do this.

LIAM. It's the company's policy.

BRIAN. Computer says no.

ALICE. Did you know they were going to do this, Liam?

LIAM. No.

ALICE. I don't believe you.

LIAM. I didn't know.

ALICE. Fuck off. That's a fucking lie.

LIAM. Can someone get Alice some water?

    BRIAN *goes off.*

ALICE. I don't want water.

LIAM. You need water.

ALICE. I don't want water.

LIAM. You reek of booze, Alice.

ALICE. You reek of shit.

LIAM. I'll speak to Michael and Alan in finance.

COLETTE. Thank you.

LIAM. Good. Great.

*Beat.*

*He doesn't move.*

ALICE. Do it now.

LIAM. I've got work to do, Alice. We've got work to do.

ALICE. This is work.

LIAM. I'll do it later.

ALICE. Pick up the phone and phone finance or whatever and say this isn't happening.

COLETTE. It isn't right.

ALICE. It's not human.

*Beat.*

ROB. What's going on, Liam?          .

LIAM. Nothing. It's just complex.

ALICE. He's scared.

LIAM. I'm not. (*Beat.*) I don't think there's anything I can do.

ALICE. How do you know?

LIAM. It's just the way it is.

ROB. But you have to try, mate.

LIAM. I wish I could.

ALICE. He's worried about his job.

ROB. If you don't do this, mate.

ALICE. I'll call them, I don't care.

LIAM. Don't call them. You'll get yourself fired.

ALICE. You've signed off on this, haven't you?

*Beat.*

Hamster?

*Beat.*

LIAM. Money's tight. You have no idea how tight.

BRIAN. About as tight as your little asshole I imagine.

ROB. Nice one, Bri.

LIAM. We're in trouble.

ALICE. I don't give a fuck. You shouldn't give a fuck.

LIAM. I know you're having a hard time, I know, we're all having a hard time but we have to keep going.

ROB. This isn't about getting on with things. I'm up for that. Move on. Life is for the living, all of that. But this is about a little bit of decency, a little bit of respect. She fell, mate. You weren't there. She was there, she was laughing, she was dancing. We were dancing and then she wasn't. She didn't even scream.

ALICE. There was no time. She was alive and then she wasn't. Just like that. Twenty seconds and then it's all gone.

ROB. I kissed her ten minutes before, ten minutes later Alice and I held her head together on the street.

ALICE. Make the call, Liam.

*Pause.*

LIAM. I will. Later.

*Beat.*

Colette, can you make everyone a tea?

COLETTE. No.

LIAM. Colette?

COLETTE. No.

LIAM. Alright, I'll do it.

*He goes over to the kitchen.*

I can't remember, did you take sugar, Colette?

COLETTE. No.

LIAM. Brian? Two for you, right.

BRIAN. Yes thank you.

LIAM. Good. So look everyone just sit down, take five. It's fine, relax. We're on a break.

ROB. Are you? Is he?

ALICE (*to* ROB). Just sit down.

LIAM. How was everyone's weekends?

*Silence.*

I know, I know. We can talk about Liz. Do you want to talk about Liz? Let's talk about Liz. We should talk about Liz.

LIAM *brings over* ALICE*'s tea.*

*She looks at it.*

*She pours it on the floor.*

Alice!

*She produces the hip flask of vodka from her bag, takes a swig and then passes it to* ROB *who drinks.*

Okay, okay.

ROB *passes it to* COLETTE, *who hesitates but then swigs.*

ROB. Brian?

BRIAN. Bottoms up.

*He takes the bottle and downs some.*

LIAM. Alright then, pass it over.

ALICE *snatches the bottle before it can reach him.*

ALICE. You've got your tea.

LIAM. Give me the bottle.

ALICE. No.

LIAM. Come on, guys, you can't drink in here.

ALICE. Who's drinking? Are you drinking, Rob?

*She hands the bottle to* ROB.

ROB. Just a spot of tea. Boss here says we're on a break.

ALICE. Brian, Colette?

BRIAN. Never touch the stuff.

LIAM. Give me the bottle, Colette, before this gets out of hand.

COLETTE.

LIAM. Give us the bottle, Colette.

COLETTE. No.

LIAM. Colette.

LIAM *grabs the bottle off* COLETTE *a bit too roughly. She falls off her chair.*

ROB. Fuck.

ALICE. Careful, Liam.

LIAM. Shit. Are you okay?

*He goes to help her up.*

ROB. What the fuck are you doing?

LIAM. I'm just trying to help.

ROB (*to* COLETTE). Are you alright? (*To* LIAM.) You pushed her.

LIAM. What, no I didn't.

ROB. You did.

LIAM. No I didn't mean to I was / just trying to –

ROB. Colette could report you for that.

COLETTE. What?

ROB. You could report Liam for that, he'd get in so much shit. Everyone saw, right?

ALICE. Yes.

LIAM. She's fine. You're fine, aren't you, Colette?

ROB. Don't answer that.

LIAM. If Duncan saw all this. I'm just trying to help you guys.

ROB. By attacking us.

COLETTE. Rob, I'm not sure about this.

*We see* DUNCAN *in the doorway.*

ROB. This is how we get some fucking justice, Col. This is going to properly get them in the shit.

DUNCAN. Hello, all. Busy, are we?

ROB. Perfect, just the man we were after.

LIAM. Duncan, can I have a word?

ROB. Liam here attacked Colette.

DUNCAN. Is this a joke?

ALICE. No he went for her.

ROB. This is deadly.

DUNCAN. Tell me what happened?

LIAM. I'm sorry, Duncan.

DUNCAN. Don't say the s-word quite yet, Liam.

LIAM. Sorry.

DUNCAN. Tell me exactly what happened?

ROB. Well, Liam. / Lost his –

DUNCAN. Colette can speak for herself, can't she?

COLETTE. Yes.

DUNCAN. She's rather good at it actually. I've been meaning to congratulate you on your sales.

COLETTE. Thank you.

DUNCAN. What happened?

COLETTE. Well, we were arguing about the payslips and then Liam grabbed the bottle from me.

DUNCAN. Sorry, what bottle?

COLETTE. This one here.

    DUNCAN *takes the bottle/hip flask.*

DUNCAN. The one full of vodka?

    *Beat.*

    And who was drinking?

    *Beat.*

    No, come on, who was drinking?

    *Beat.*

    Whose is this? This isn't a joke, this is a place of work.

ALICE. It's mine.

COLETTE. No we all had a drink but it was because / you docked us our pay.

DUNCAN. You all had a drink? In the day? At work?

ROB. That's not the point. The point is Liam pushed Colette.

DUNCAN. Was Liam drinking?

LIAM. No, I was trying to stop them.

ROB. Colette bashed her head. After Liz I would have thought that's the kind of thing you'd be worried about.

DUNCAN. Colette, listen to me. You can make a complaint but you should know this is very serious. This would be very serious for Liam. We take this kind of accusation very seriously. There would need to be an investigation, Liam would probably have to be suspended, meanwhile we'd have to look into this drinking culture. There may well be consequences there. Is it really worth it?

LIAM. Please, Colette, you're leaving anyway.

ALICE. You're leaving?

COLETTE. I don't know yet.

LIAM. She's got a new job.

DUNCAN. Very nice.

ALICE. You didn't tell me.

COLETTE (*to* ALICE). I'm sorry.

DUNCAN. Well no we'd be sorry to lose you although perhaps your new employers might have concerns about this drinking.

ROB. You can't do that. You can't give bad references.

DUNCAN. No one's talking about references but there would need to be a tribunal.

ROB. You can't just threaten us. We all saw.

DUNCAN. Did you see, Brian?

BRIAN *hesitates*.

ROB. Come on, Bri. Back of the net.

BRIAN.

DUNCAN. It's hard to be certain of anything when you're all a bit drunk, isn't it?

*Beat.*

Fine. Right, Colette, I just want you to know that I will absolutely support any decision you make and if you want to make a report against Liam I would absolutely support that.

LIAM. Colette –

COLETTE. No don't worry. I'm fine. I don't want to make a report, it was just an accident. Liam didn't mean it. And we didn't mean it. We're sorry about all this. Can we just leave it.

DUNCAN. Of course. Good. That's a relief.

ROB. Wow. Wow. This is just. You're just. You're perfect. I'm done. I'm out.

*ROB lashes out or perhaps he doesn't, perhaps he just picks up his coat.*

ALICE. Rob?

BRIAN. Where are you going? Don't go.

ROB. I'm out.

*He exits.*

*Beat.*

DUNCAN. Fine. Come upstairs once everything is sorted. Back to work, everyone.

LIAM. Back to work, everyone.

*They move out towards the work space.* ALICE *starts making a noise.*

*Blackout.*

**ACT FIVE**

**Spring**

*The green room or office.* LIAM *in a suit.* ALICE *has also made an effort.*

LIAM. Come in.

   ALICE *enters.*

   Hi, Alice.

ALICE. Hi.

LIAM. How are you?

ALICE. Oh you know.

LIAM. Right.

ALICE. No, not like that. I'm okay actually, I'm good. I'm feeling better.

LIAM. Good.

ALICE. How are you?

   *Beat.*

LIAM. I'm well, thank you. Thanks for asking. No one asks me that any more.

   *Pause.*

   Sit down. Please. Sorry.

   *She sits down.*

   You look better.

ALICE. Thanks. It was a bad bug.

LIAM. There's a lot going around.

ALICE. That time of year.

*Beat.*

Don't we sound funny? Like strangers. Adult strangers.

LIAM. Oh no.

ALICE. We'll be having dinner parties next.

LIAM. Nothing wrong with dinner parties.

ALICE. How are things going with, I'm sorry I've forgotten her name.

LIAM. Kate. Good. Nice. It's still early days.

ALICE. She seemed really nice. That time. I was a bit. What does she do?

LIAM. She's a nursery teacher.

ALICE. Lovely.

LIAM. And are you still seeing Rob? How is he?

ALICE. No, God no. Fuck no. Sorry. That was just a moment. Let's call it insanity. I think he's alright though. He's enjoying recruitment. He's fine. He's Rob. How is Brian without Rob?

LIAM. Yeah he's better actually. We're all doing okay. Do you hear from Colette?

ALICE. No.

LIAM. I had to hire someone else when you were off. A girl called Sanna.

ALICE. I met her. She seems good.

LIAM. She is.

ALICE. Thank you for bearing with me though.

LIAM. You went back home?

ALICE. I did.

LIAM. Did they look after you?

ALICE. My mum tried. My granny was lovely. She loved
    having me there and wanted to spoil me but her back is too
    bad so I spent most of my time looking after her.

LIAM. Shit.

ALICE. No, I think that helped.

LIAM. You're feeling better.

ALICE. Yes.

LIAM. Good.

ALICE. I still feel sad. I still have my days.

LIAM. Do you?

ALICE. Not as bad. I'm not as bad.

    *Pause.*

LIAM. What's the plan then?

ALICE. What do you mean?

LIAM. What happens next?

ALICE. I don't know, do I? Do you?

LIAM. I know more than I did.

ALICE. Good for you.

LIAM. And the drinking?

ALICE. Fine.

LIAM. What?

ALICE. Right. No good let's talk about it. I'm drinking less.

LIAM. But you're still drinking.

ALICE. I feel much better.

    *Beat.*

    I'm sorry. I'm sorry I called you that time.

LIAM. Don't worry.

ALICE. I'm a mean drunk.

LIAM. You are a bit. But I might have been a mean boss.

ALICE. You weren't mean.

LIAM. I think I might have been.

ALICE. It was Duncan.

LIAM. Duncan has a boss too.

What about the music?

ALICE. I don't want to talk about music. It's boring. I like
singing. I like playing guitar. I can still do that. I don't have
to be a star. I don't even know what that means really.

LIAM. So what will you do?

ALICE. I'll work it out. I need to earn some money first.

LIAM. Are you sure you want to come back?

ALICE. I don't want to come back obviously.

LIAM. Obviously?

ALICE. I didn't mean it in a bad way.

LIAM. Not sure how you can mean it in a good way.

ALICE. It's just a money job, isn't it? Don't go funny, hamster.

LIAM. I'm not a hamster.

*Beat.*

ALICE. I'll only be back for a bit and I'll work hard, I just need
the cash urgently.

LIAM. Alice, you can't. You can't tell me that. You can't tell
me you're going to leave.

ALICE. But no one stays.

LIAM. I've stayed. Brian's stayed.

ALICE. I'm sorry it's just not a proper job, that's all I meant.

LIAM. You can't say that either.

ALICE. Sorry. But you've said much worse. You used to tell me to leave all the time. You said I was too good for this place. You are too good for this place. You said.

LIAM. I know. The problem is management want to keep Sanna. She's got a great way with customers, her sales are good. People like her. It just doesn't make sense to fire her. And the tricky thing is we can't afford to hire anyone else, we're having to make cutbacks.

ALICE. But you promised I'd still have my job after my break.

LIAM. I know but you were gone for six weeks.

ALICE. You all told me to go.

LIAM. You weren't well.

ALICE. I know.

LIAM. And now you're feeling better.

ALICE. I am.

LIAM. I'm glad.

*Pause.*

ALICE. Are you firing me, Liam?

LIAM. No I'm just letting you go.

*Blackout.*

*The End.*

**www.nickhernbooks.co.uk**

 facebook.com/nickhernbooks

twitter.com/nickhernbooks